THE RIGHT USE
OF MONEY

Edited by David Darton

FRIENDS PROVIDENT
Foundation

First published in Great Britain in July 2004 by

The Policy Press
University of Bristol
Fourth Floor, Beacon House
Queen's Road
Bristol BS8 1QU

Tel +44 (0)117 331 4054
Fax +44 (0)117 331 4093
e-mail tpp-info@bristol.ac.uk
www.policypress.org.uk

© Friends Provident Foundation 2004

British Library Cataloguing in Publication Data
A catalogue record for this book is available from the British Library

Library of Congress Cataloging-in-Publication Data
A catalog record for this book has been requested

ISBN 1 86134 616 6 paperback

David Darton is a freelance consultant and part-time Strategy and
Research Director at the Equal Opportunities Commission.

Cover design by Qube Design Associates, Bristol
Front cover: photograph kindly supplied by Sean Malyon
Printed and bound in Great Britain by Hobbs the Printers, Southampton

Contents

Foreword

Friends Provident was founded in 1832 and is now a major financial institution. When it changed its status from a mutual society to a public limited company in 2001, the Board decided to create a charitable foundation for existing community support and developing new ways to contribute towards a better world.

The new Foundation has an endowment of £20 million to fund work of benefit to the community, continuing a tradition of almost two centuries of community involvement by the company and its staff. We therefore commissioned this book to help inform us about some of the issues we should consider in our management of the endowment and to stimulate creative thought on the part of those applying for funds. We also hope that it will contribute to a wider national debate on 'the right use of money' as society continues to become more and more affluent.

Careful thought about the use of money and resources has been a traditional concern of the company since its inception by members of the Religious Society of Friends (Quakers). In conducting its business, it has always embraced Quaker values – recognising the significance of each individual and striving for social justice, peace, equality, simplicity, truth and integrity – and, in the business context, fair dealing. Two practical examples have been the lead that Friends Provident took in developing concepts of stewardship and responsible engagement when conducting business.

In 1984, when there was widespread concern over apartheid in South Africa and, nearer home, unemployment, urban decay and poverty, Friends Provident considered how a financial services company could use its resources – financial and human – to contribute towards a more harmonious society. The result was the UK's first unit trust that invested in companies whose products and services contributed towards a more peaceful and harmonious world: the Stewardship Trust. This worked through advice from an independent panel that assessed the positive and negative features of companies. The stewardship concept has flourished since then and been replicated by other companies recognising that many people wish their money to be used for well-being rather than harming people and the environment. The implication is that money management means more than maximising financial returns – there is also a real issue about how and where money is invested and used, and from where profits are generated.

Friends Provident also took a lead in working with companies to change and improve corporate actions. Since April 2000 this proactive stance, Responsible Engagement Overlay (REO), has met with real success. Examples of REO include improving working conditions in 'developing' countries in which a company operates, or reducing environmental degradation or supporting minority groups in their workplace.

We recognise the need to build on these successes and be innovative in developing other approaches and mechanisms for ensuring the 'right use of money'. We therefore sought articles for this book from a wide spectrum of opinion formers and thinkers in this area. This collection of essays is the result. We hope that it will stimulate innovation in our monetary system, institutions and instruments; in the practical methods for ethical principles to underpin our use of money; and in the approaches that will empower, rather than entrap, the recipients of money. We shall use the ideas presented here to help us shape and focus our grant-making activities.

Brian Sweetland, Danielle Walker, John Whitney and Lyn Wilson
Friends Provident Charitable Foundation

Scope of this book and acknowledgements

As the world continues to become ever more interconnected and complex, the decisions we take when spending and investing money not only affect ourselves, our neighbours and our local community, but also millions of others with whom we will have no direct contact. International organisations, governments, businesses, voluntary organisations and individuals take decisions that are often at a huge distance from those on whom they will have an impact.

This has been true for some considerable time, but have our institutional arrangements and our personal approaches to the way we use money kept up? So that we can be sure that our spending and investment contributes positively to our communities, to our economic welfare and to our environment, a national debate on the ways to ensure this seems timely.

With this in mind, a wide range of people with differing perspectives were contacted and asked to set out their initial thoughts on how we might increase the chances of money being used in positive ways. Inevitably, not all were able to respond and not every perspective is represented here. In particular, we only got a response from the Conservative Party, although responses from other parties were requested. We are also conscious that in this collection only one contributor, Moraene Roberts, has experienced poverty directly; we have not therefore been able to do justice to the perspectives of people who are disadvantaged by a lack of resources. Continuing to develop creative ideas from new perspectives is something that we hope others will take on over the next few years.

Nevertheless, the contributions that make up this book contain a rich and diverse set of ideas that should stimulate thought, debate, and hopefully some action. My biggest thanks clearly go to all those who have taken the time and trouble to provide such thought-provoking essays.

But also, my great appreciation goes to the Trustees of the new Friends Provident Charitable Foundation. Not only have they initiated and funded this enterprise, and committed themselves to ongoing consideration of the right use of money in their grant making, they have also been enormously supportive to me personally during the process of drawing all this material together.

Over the years, I have worked with The Policy Press on many publications and as usual their professional approach and enthusiasm has made a huge difference. Finally, thanks to my partner, Colin, for putting up with the late nights that have been necessary to fit this project around my other work and family commitments; and to my employer, the Equal Opportunities Commission, for its flexible working arrangements that allow me to take on exciting projects such as this one and still have a life outside work!

David Darton

List of contributors

Pierre Calame has been head of the Charles Leopold Mayer Foundation since 1986.

Church of England Doctrine Commission

Philip Collins is Director of the Social Market Foundation.

Niall Cooper is a co-founder and chair of the Debt on our Doorstep campaign.

Jonathan Dale lives and works in Ordsall, Salford, helping a group of tenants to manage their social housing.

David Darton is a freelance consultant for a range of private and public clients in business strategy, research strategy and communications and is part-time Strategy and Research Director at the Equal Opportunities Commission.

Jed Emerson is a Lecturer in Business at Stanford University Graduate School of Business, and a Senior Fellow of the William and Flora Hewlett Foundation and the David and Lucile Packard Foundation.

Ram Gidoomal is an author, entrepreneur and former UK Group Chief Executive of the Inlaks Group.

Charles Handy is a writer and broadcaster.

Julia Neuberger is former chief executive of the King's Fund (1997-2004), a former member of the Committee on Standards in Public Life (2001-4) and a trustee of the Booker Foundation. She was awarded a DBE in the 2004 New Year's Honours and created a life peer in 2004.

Stephen O'Brien, formerly shadow Paymaster General and Secretary to the Treasury, is currently the Shadow Secretary of State for Industry.

Matthew Pike is Director of the Scarman Trust.

Moraene Roberts is an activist with the human rights-based organisation, ATD Fourth World.

Dorothy Rowe is a psychologist and writer.

Tony Stoller is a broadcasting regulator and senior manager in both media and retailing.

Polly Toynbee is a political and social commentator for *The Guardian*.

Part One: Overview

1

Towards a 'right use of money'

David Darton

David Darton is a consultant for a range of private and public clients
in business strategy, research strategy and communications, and is
part of a consortium providing media training. He also works as
Strategy and Research Director for the Equal Opportunities
Commission and is writing his first novel, a thriller. His earlier career
was centrally concerned with money: as Senior Economist for the
Korea Exchange Bank and Korean Ministry of Finance based in Seoul
and then as a Founder Director of the strategic business consultancy,
the Henley Centre for Forecasting, which subsequently became part
of the international marketing group, WPP. More recently he spent
ten years as Communications/Strategy Director at the
Joseph Rowntree Foundation.

"Such a complicated thing, then, is money. It is our livelihood, the way
we pay for our bread and butter; it is the way we create work for other
people; it is a measure of success, whether you store it in a bank or
spend it on unnecessary things; it is a consolation prize for missing out
on your vocation; it can even be an excuse for not following that
vocation.... No wonder we get confused. No wonder that so many
make money the point of life rather than the means of life. It was not
meant to be that way when it was first devised as the universal
mechanism of exchange." (Charles Handy, Chapter Nine, this volume)

T his book is about money. Not about how to make it, but about how to use it and use it well. This is not easy: not only Charles Handy, but also many other contributors to this book note the complexity of money, its multiple roles and the resulting difficulties in determining the right use of money. It is hardly surprising then that the authors of these short chapters, left completely free to explore the topic from their own perspectives, have adopted a wide variety of starting points and styles.

The eclectic nature of the contributions helps us take a fresh, creative look at the issues. What is especially fascinating, however, are some common threads that weave between many of the pieces. Collectively these can be summarised as philanthropy, empowerment, stewardship, transparency. From these themes, the authors identify a number of approaches and practical mechanisms for improving the use of money and achieving social change. These are summarised more fully in Part Five of this book.

Philanthropy

Many of the chapters urge us to use money for the benefit of others. Philip Collins (Chapter Ten, this volume) uses the term 'philanthropy' explicitly in the context of saying that this is a reasonable motivation for corporate social responsibility. In short, it is not all about the business case. A number of contributors also talk about the need for companies to recognise a range of stakeholders other than just shareholders, although often feel that, in the long term, consideration of all stakeholders is in the shareholders' interest anyway. Julia Neuberger (Chapter Seven) is explicit that what is required are measures to instil a philanthropic (or, in her terms, 'giving') culture throughout society, particularly at the individual level.

A major theme, therefore, is that one way to use money constructively is philanthropy: advancing societal development through the arts and sport, and so on, but primarily in the sense of helping disadvantaged or vulnerable people. A few of the chapters are specific: this means 'poor' people, either in this country or in developing countries. Matthew Pike (Chapter Fifteen) puts this case most starkly:

Lack of money ruins people's lives.

Niall Cooper (Chapter Sixteen) talks of the imperative to help disadvantaged people, and Polly Toynbee (Chapter Eleven) is particularly concerned with society's duty – through government – to redistribute resources to those on low incomes:

The West's most equal societies are the happiest, the most unequal the most unhappy.

Empowerment

Many contributors consider that social change is not solved just through redistribution – that is, simply through 'throwing money' at people. Rather, it is how you do it that matters. There is a strong sense that monetary processes are vitally important. Stephen O'Brien (Chapter Five) suggests that encouraging enterprise is key; indeed, he feels that the balance between free markets and state redistribution should be moved more towards the US model (as opposed to the European one). Where government does intervene, redistributing resources and providing services, it should be on the basis of being 'people-oriented' – that is, in governmental terms, replacing central control and targets with a more decentralised approach.

A number of contributors also pick up the theme of being 'people-oriented'. Matthew Pike (Chapter Fifteen) believes the main issue for poor people is a sense of 'helplessness', not just lack of money. He emphasises the need to listen carefully to those who are the recipients of philanthropy and really understand their worldview; that is, the 'view from the ground', about what will help. Indeed, Dorothy Rowe (Chapter Thirteen) suggests that, if those giving money fail to make the effort to understand the recipients' point of view, tragedy can follow.

Moraene Roberts (Chapter Twelve) says that services will be improved if the resources are there to spend the time necessary to developing "real knowledge of a person's struggles and efforts and the problems that bring them to the attention of statutory agencies". A number of others are also concerned with the idea of investing in communities in ways that help overcome helplessness. To do

---

5

this, one needs to "develop the assets [of communities] in the round", recognising more intangible forms of assets, such as cultural ones or organisational and knowledge capital as well as the more tangible ones, such as buildings and facilities. We are reminded also of the importance of investing in 'can-do' people, and Ram Gidoomal (Chapter Fourteen) highlights in particular the need to respond to different cultural requirements if one really is to empower people.

Stewardship

Empowering philanthropy, however, needs to be set in the context of the use of all the world's resources. Polly Toynbee (Chapter Eleven) notes that most things that make a real difference to people's quality of life are collectively provided – from transport to parks to litter collection. This sense of the interconnectedness of individuals and institutions and the importance of marshalling the world's resources to the long-term benefit of all is picked up in many of the contributions to this volume.

> The world population is soon to be 8 billion.... [The vital need will be] to live in harmony and dignity, while making sure that the balances of the biosphere are not destroyed. (Pierre Calame, Chapter Three, this volume)

The importance of taking into account environmental and social factors, as well as economic ones, in investment decisions is emphasised time and time again. In particular, Jed Emerson says "the right use of money is quite simply those strategies that seek to maximise our capacity for leveraging our total assets in pursuit of the full value we seek to create" (Chapter Two). Full value includes environmental and social value as well as economic value.

Transparency

In order to allow effective stewardship of resources for the common good, a number of contributions to this volume pick up the need for our monetary and economic systems to be more transparent –

to be better at signalling the true costs and benefits of our consumption and investment than currently is sometimes the case. Tony Stoller (Chapter Six) says that the lack of transparency and adequate price signals often hides the links between our spending and morality. The extracts from the Church of England's think tank, the Doctrine Commission (Chapter Eight), also underline that money and prices no longer directly reflect the trade that relates to human need or suffering and is removed from the sphere of human values. This sense that monetary value does not reflect the true social costs of production and distribution, hiding ethical issues from the consumer, is apparent in a number of contributions. Jonathan Dale (Chapter Four) suggests that we need to completely rethink our concept of value (and indeed need to replace our most general indicator of economic value, GDP, with an index of *sustainable* economic welfare). The sustainability aspect would make social and environmental costs more transparent.

The theme of transparency is also picked up in other contexts. For example, Polly Toynbee (Chapter Eleven) writes that we need greater transparency about the criteria we use to set wages. She notes that nowadays the highest paid in an organisation are often given remuneration packages 200 times the amount of the lowest paid, compared to a norm of around ten times in the 1970s. In the absence of transparency about why some resources cost more than others, she questions whether such high remuneration is a 'right use of money'.

Julia Neuberger (Chapter Seven) would like to see earmarking of some income tax for charitable giving. In general, there is a feeling among many of the contributors that our complex systems do not allow us to see clearly where our money is going and therefore the implications of our decisions.

An agenda for social change

So, we need a more philanthropic approach, but one that is enabling and born of a recognition of our interdependence with each other and with the environment and one that illuminates the effects of our own action. Such an approach must be grounded in greater transparency to increase our understanding of the seemingly mysterious global monetary system that ties us inextricably together. This leads the contributors to suggest approaches and mechanisms for the use of money that would create social change. Indeed, many of them implicitly or explicitly define the right use of money as having the purpose of positive social change.

As Ram Gidoomal (Chapter Fourteen) says, social change comes from changed people. In different ways, the chapters suggest that this will require people's motivations to be changed through a variety of means: making the true costs and benefits of transactions more visible (transparent); making the concept of social justice attractive again; and persuading people that philanthropic activity, which empowers vulnerable people, is in everyone's enlightened self-interest. Many note that this is more possible when people take a longer-term perspective than is often the case in consumer and money markets today.

The apparent (especially short-term) contradiction between wealth creation and philanthropic activity is noted, especially by Stephen O'Brien (Chapter Five) and Charles Handy (Chapter Nine). However, many believe this to be less true in the long term, particularly if wealth creation is interpreted to mean more than the development of the relatively narrow range of assets that companies and governments often consider. Even those contributors who emphasise the value of the market, recognise society's needs for non-market relationships either in terms of compensating for the undesirable effects of markets left completely to their own devices, or in areas where market relationships are not the best ways of allocating resources. Pierre Calame (Chapter Three) in particular defines the types of goods and services that he believes should be transacted and valued by means other than market ones. And Moraene Roberts (Chapter Twelve) notes the importance of valuing contributions other than paid employment.

All the contributors to this book ultimately work from the (very likely) premise that both markets and other methods of allocating resources will continue to coexist. Three broad starting points are used for thinking about what use of money would deliver positive social change in this mixed economy. The first is that there need to be fundamental adaptations to our financial and economic systems. The second is that clearer moral or ethical principles should drive our decisions. The third is that we need to think through what sorts of expenditure would really be empowering. The remainder of this book is divided into three parts that reflect these starting points. Essays are placed within them according to which starting point is emphasised, although this division is sometimes slightly arbitrary, as this organising perspective was not imposed on the contributors at the start of writing.

From all these starting points a wide range of possible approaches for the future are identified. Over the coming years, some of them may contribute to the shape of how government, business, voluntary organisations and individuals use their money to deliver positive social change.

Part Two: The role of money in 21st-century Britain's economy

The authors in this section are concerned with the intrinsic nature of money within Britain's financial systems. For them, the 'right use of money' depends on recognising how money operates in a modern economy. Many point out that money and other financial instruments are too narrow a measure of value, dealing only with economic value and, thereby, inadequately measuring social or environmental costs. As a result, investment decisions are in danger of only considering economic growth or financial gain. Many are also concerned that money (and prices) are too distant from the realities of the trade that underlies them. As a consequence, purchase and investment decisions can be made without appreciation of their full implications.

The failure of money to adequately reflect social or environmental value is a central theme of **Jed Emerson**. He suggests that the 'right use of money' will only occur if investment decisions are made on the basis of assessing 'full value' returns; that is, the blended value of economic gain, social gain and environmental gain.

Pierre Calame also identifies the simultaneous meeting of economic, environmental and social need as the greatest challenge. He feels that currency systems and other economic institutions fail to meet this challenge. To correct this failure, he suggests investigating how the overall monetary system and its governance need to be changed. He feels that local or regional 'territories' will gradually become more important players, relative to international corporations in meeting combined economic, environmental and social requirements.

Jonathan Dale highlights that money in today's complex world is often very distant from the true nature of production and trade. In particular, he is concerned that prices do not reflect true social costs, so that ethical issues are hidden from the consumer. At the same time, companies are accountable only to shareholders and not to the other stakeholders affected socially and economically by their activities.

Finally, **Stephen O'Brien** picks up the problem of decisions being far too removed from the realities of trade and the needs of people in their local communities. He suggests that governments' 'right use of money' should foster free enterprise and wealth creation and use people-focused techniques: localism over centralism; diversity over rigid targets and controls.

2

A 'full investment' approach

Jed Emerson

Jed Emerson is a Lecturer in Business at Stanford University Graduate School of Business and a Senior Fellow of the William and Flora Hewlett Foundation and the David and Lucile Packard Foundation. He was also the Bloomberg Senior Research Fellow in Philanthropy at Harvard Business School. His current work centres on the Blended Value Proposition (www.blendedvalue.org) which explores the intersects of economic, social and environmental value creation by both for-profit and non-profit firms.

What is money?

It is often said that money is the root of all evil, but the original words state that it is the *love* of money that is the root of all evil. The point is an important one, for in truth money is simply a tool, a mechanism, a measure of economic performance. In and of itself, money is morally neutral. Yet how wealth is pursued, how money is managed and the way in which much of 'modern' society tends to focus on money as an ultimate measure of worth are the true questions upon which we should focus our attentions.

Money is simply a proxy for economic value and a way to 'keep score'. However, it is a grossly blunt instrument of measurement that is inherently flawed: that is, it does not truly capture the full measure of worth created through the application of our life assets. Money claims to be a measure of value, yet value itself consists not simply of economic returns, but rather a blended return emanating from a mix of economic, social and environmental components. In truth, value may not be bifurcated – one half doing well, the other doing badly – in the same way that a DNA strand does not naturally fall apart if it is to achieve its full purpose in building a whole being. It is only the mutant strand that is not whole or does not fulfil the full promise of its potential. Therefore, we cannot consider money without also considering how money can be used to maximise economic performance, as well as social and environmental impacts.

The institutions that channel money

The same holds true of the organisations that make use of or 'channel' money and those that put it to use. Companies cannot be viewed solely as engines of economic value creation and non-governmental organisations (NGOs) generators of social worth. Indeed, contrary to popular opinion, corporations are not necessarily the 'bad guys' and NGOs the white knights, because, in truth, for-profit firms create social and environmental value and non-profit firms have economic worth. Just as value is a composite of three elements and is not purely good or bad, there is no 'pure' firm that engages in simply one or the other type of value creation activity.

We use money, in the form of capital, as the fuel by which we pursue value creation by organisations. Our capital falls along an investment plane: investments that seek a mix of returns ranging from purely social to purely financial, with gradations of grey in between. Our investment instruments range from grants to recoverable grants, to concessionary rate loans and notes, to market-rate instruments seeking only financial return. Yet our goal and purpose for applying these instruments of investment should be to engage in full-value investing that maximises total blended value. We tend to view the institutions that manage these investment instruments as being discrete (for example, foundations make grants, while equity funds make market-rate investments), yet in truth our investment strategies may reflect the same blend as is present in the nature of value itself.

For example, the Abell Foundation of Baltimore, Maryland (US), is a grant-making foundation concerned with job training for inner-city youth. Yet the investment of the foundation's corpus (which most foundations usually manage only for the generation of financial return) is invested in companies the foundation determines to be creating positive social value through the location of production facilities. The Abell Foundation maintains a venture capital fund as part of its diversified investment strategy, but as a condition of investing in a given company the term sheet includes provisions for job creation in the inner city. In this way, the foundation's trustees are pursuing full, 'blended value' in fulfilment of their fiduciary responsibilities and the organisation's institutional mission.

The appropriate role of grant-making institutions is not simply to engage in grant making, but rather to pursue strategies that use grants as a means to an end. The most relevant 21st-century philanthropy seeks to manage a foundation's total assets in pursuit of full value creation. As might be expected, the appropriate balance of this 'blended' portfolio of investments will differ from foundation to foundation, but the fundamental truth remains.

Those assets available to foundations include such tools as grants, loans and equity investments which when managed in concert with the foundation's social assets of policy positions, staff expertise and other 'non-grant' investments make up the total tool box of instruments that may be applied in pursuit of its purpose and value creation potential.

The dissemination of such approaches is not limited to the foundation community, but is also increasingly seen in how mainstream, for-profit firms are managed and is also present in the emerging practice of social enterprise by NGOs. The task is not to convert the unwashed by convincing businesses to be more socially aware or NGOs to function in a more business-like manner, but rather to explore the true nature of value creation efforts within a host of institutional contexts.

As we see the evolving demands being placed upon companies attempting to thrive in global markets, we see managers being forced by those markets to perform not simply on the basis of economic value creation, but social and environmental measures of worth as well. If current trends continue, in the decades to come the successful for-profit firm will be one that returns value to both shareholder and stakeholder alike. Those that do not will lose the license to operate and be punished by being limited to only those geographic markets willing to allow others to continue to profit economically at the expense of the environmental and social well-being of local communities and urban centres.

In the same way, the successful NGO is not the one that attempts to hold blindly to acts of pure charity, but rather one that uses its charitable activities in concert with the latest business practices in order to maximise the full value of its efforts in order to achieve the greatest good. For example, in the US the non-profit sector constitutes approximately 7% of the country's gross domestic product (GDP). What would happen if we simply managed the *cash flow* of those funds with reference to the larger social and environmental values of our sector? Were all the NGOs in the US to manage their accounts through community development banks, it would create a huge economic force capable of a great many things, yet we think of ourselves as 'charities' and by so doing leave our economic value on the table for others. So, we keep our checking and savings accounts in mainstream, capital market institutions which manage those funds with no reference to our social or environmental agenda and by so doing allow our own resources to support and contribute to many of the very problems we claim to be addressing through the rest of our organisational assets.

The 'right use of money' is quite simply those strategies that seek to maximise our capacity for leveraging our total assets in pursuit of the full value we seek to create. It is not about philanthropy, but rather social change, and as such our financial resources must be invested in accordance with our overall mission. Foundations should provide NGOs with concessionary rate loans in order to assist them in acquiring the buildings they use in order to build long-term assets that may in turn be leveraged in other ways. Our financial corpus must be managed through for-profit firms with a commitment to maximising the full value we seek in the form of job creation and sustainable business practices. And our grant-making practices themselves must seek to build long-term capacity and maximum effectiveness for those NGOs we do choose to support.

The 'right use of money' is not executed in the form of simply charitable giving, but rather in fulfilment of social investment practices writ large. The total assets of our institutions must be leveraged to create the greatest impacts in pursuit of our overall missions. The actual focus of our interests can and should be many and diverse. It does not matter whether we target community development, youth services or health issues, in that, if we approach whatever specific topic we select with an awareness of the need to mobilise the full set of assets available to us, we will, virtually by definition, seek to draw upon the talents of our elders and the energies of our youth as best applied through both for-profit and not-for-profit organisations. The market place of ideas and needs and interests is wide and varied enough that, as long as each investing entity seeks to pursue a strategy of full value investing by mobilising their total assets, we will find ourselves focusing upon what we need to as our neighbour focuses upon what they feel called to address. Together, the collective effort of our labours will be to change the world and how life is experienced by the diverse members of our community.

Quite simply, there is no single, 'most important' area in which we are called to work, but rather we are simply called to work in the various areas we feel drawn to, but to do so as part of a larger community of actors investing our assets in the pursuit and creation of full value.

3

Meeting economic, environmental and social challenges simultaneously

Pierre Calame

Pierre Calame has been head of the Charles Leopold Mayer Foundation since 1986. The Foundation explores alternatives to the way things are currently done, including exploring new economic paradigms and considering ethics for the 21st century, the future of money and the management of natural resources. He is closely concerned with the management of the Foundation's assets, which in itself raises important financial market issues. Previous to his present position, he was a senior civil servant for 20 years, including being faced with the severe industrial and economic crisis of Northern France in the 1970s, an experience that particularly affects his thinking about the economy and money.

U p until the 1960s and the 1970s, before the West became fully aware of the human and environmental damages caused by the Soviet Union and China, we had a ready-made alternative to the terrible effects of unbridled capitalism and currency. It was called Socialism. The fall of the Berlin Wall and the subsequent conversion of the former Socialist countries, or at least of most of them, to capitalism (often a particularly radical capitalism) eliminated the utopian alternative. But, in the process, they did not eliminate the very real negative effects of an increasingly globalised society, where the concentration of capital and an unchecked scientific and technological development make the rich increasingly richer and the poor increasingly useless; where 20% of the world's population consume more than 80% of the world's natural resources; and where, despite the very weak development of a significant part of the planet, we consume yearly more than one and a half of what the same planet is able to reproduce.

So, the collapse of Communism has left the West facing all of its responsibilities: it now has to invent, on the basis of its own foundations, a radical alternative that will allow the world's soon-to-be eight billion human beings to live in harmony and dignity and at the same time to make sure that the main balances of the biosphere are not completely destroyed, with all that this implies for the future of our human adventure. Searching for such an alternative and stating that another world is possible are therefore not simply matters for philanthropists: elementary lucidity tells us that this is the very condition for the long-term survival of humankind. Searching for these alternatives forces us to take a fresh look at the foundations of our present system, and in particular at three of its most manifest aspects: the market, its currency, and its corporations, and their respective roles. To do so, we naturally have to question the historical foundations of our systems so we are not trapped inside the systems of thought generated by force of habit and conventionality and by what is largely assumed to be 'evident'.

This can be illustrated with a few anecdotes. I shall therefore begin by relating five experiences that helped me in my own questioning.

Local currency to connect idle hands and unmet needs

First, in the 1970s, I was a senior civil servant in France working for the Ministry of Town and Country Development, in charge of a region in the north of France called Valenciennes, which had 400,000 inhabitants. The wealth of the region was due to its coalmines, the iron and steel industry, and the heavy metallurgy that had been developed in the 19th and early 20th centuries.

Starting in the 1960s, the coalmines were rapidly closed down, the iron and steel industries moved to the coast so they could use cheaper and richer ore that came from the other side of the world, and the heavy metallurgy waned, throwing the whole region into a huge industrial, moral, cultural, economic, and political crisis. And although it continued to survive thanks to the workers' pensions, it was left with an uncertain future, a practically unskilled working population, and a particularly unattractive environment made of industrial remains. With a constantly rising unemployment rate peaking at 30%, I could plainly see the absurdity of the situation: idle hands, unused energy, and quantities of unmet needs. To me, the first aim of the economy (and also its legitimacy) was to use the unused energy to meet the unmet needs. I could clearly see that our classic economy, consolidated by the social redistribution organised by the Welfare State, redistribution which was socially right but which in this type of region acted as a sort of palliative care before certain death, did not reflect this basic definition of the economy. And that is how, without knowing that for the same reasons, and at a time when the period of constant post-war growth in Europe was ending, the same ideas were cropping up elsewhere, I suggested to the local elected officials that they create 'local currency'. They were quite taken aback, and instead of considering the proposal, they wondered whether I was in my right mind. I did not press the issue at the time, but just as Galileo had to retract his ideas before the Saint Inquisition, I could not help repeating to myself: "But we have to find a solution, and the solution includes organising exchanges at other levels than that of the Single European Market".

Moving toward two-dimensional currency

My second story takes place about 10 years later. Our Foundation (that is, the Charles Leopold Mayer Foundation) had decided to back a group of French-speaking intellectuals, the Vézelay Group, to do some in-depth thinking on the world's disparities. The focus of the group's concerns was the disparity between the desire to consume and the planet's capacity to provide everyone with enough resources to do so. Or, as Gandhi said, "There is enough in the world for all our needs, but never enough for one man's greed". The most obvious response at the time was austerity: "Consume so that enough is left over for everyone else". Following that line of reasoning, however, led me to a second obstacle: I do not only consume natural resources; I also and most of all consume the fruit of other people's work, knowledge, and know-how. If living is simply trying to make do without other people, all this does is reinforce the movement I was otherwise denouncing, thanks to which today's reality is not so much the exploitation of the poor by the rich as the even more dramatic fact that the rich can mostly get by without resorting to the poor at all. At that point I understood that we had to look for the solution elsewhere, in the very use and the nature of currency.

Allow me to explain. Currency has several functions: unit of account, means of payment, and store of value. This is so obvious to us that we no longer ever question the need, or not, for these three functions to be assigned to one and the same tool. Added to this is the fact that after the Second World War, we had to find new taxation bases and one of them, the value added tax (VAT), turned out to be particularly convenient and was broadly applied. The property of VAT is to tax human work at each successive production stage. The result is that when we buy something, we are giving equal value to the consumption of non-renewable natural resources and to that of human work, with a preference to taxing that which we should be developing, that is, human work, rather than natural resources, which we should in fact be sparing. Generalisation of VAT, however, has shown the concrete possibility of following the whole of activities through the taxing system. We can actually 'trace' within a product that we buy in a store, the part corresponding to non-renewable resources and the part corresponding to human work.

I then said to myself that, if instead of reasoning with the idea of currency as a single value, we reasoned with the idea of currency as having two components (that is, the natural-resources component and the human-work component), we would be able to develop a responsible form of consumption, one that would take environmental balances into account as well as the interdependence that is necessary for social cohesion, and thus be able to tax the quantities of natural resources that we consume, and perhaps later to fix quotas for them. Failing tools to measure this with, we are groping blindly into the future. Take the case of fair trade or fair tourism, for instance. Such trade and such tourism are only fair for a very small part of what is really the value of what we buy! There is a greater contribution to the payment of the raw material itself or, in the case of tourism, a greater consideration of the local population in our expenses, but in fact all of this amounts to no more than 10% (or, at best 20%) of the value of the product.

Currency and corporations: who will be the main social actor at the end of the 21st century?

The next story came to me from a historical outlook. In 1989, France celebrated the bicentennial of the French Revolution. Many historical studies were published for the occasion. I was especially struck by one of them. It observed that the fathers of the French Revolution had given enormous thought to the nation, power sharing, the role of the elected officials of the people, and to the state, but that they had absolutely failed to perceive and conceptualise what was in fact the reality rising before their very eyes: the company. At that time, I had been reflecting on how corporations, as we knew them then – organised on the international scale according to vertical distribution channels – were increasingly ill-suited to the reality of the problems of our time, which involved meeting economic, environmental, and social challenges simultaneously. Thereupon, I came to the conclusion that all those who saw corporations as the most powerful, or even monopolistic social actor of this 21st century were only looking at the short term and were perhaps making the same mistake in their diagnosis as the fathers of the French Revolution had done. I progressively came to the conclusion that corporations, at least as we know them now, were gradually losing their importance. Territories, and by this I mean agglomerations as well as entities made up of towns and rural territories, could very well be the most important social actors of the 21st century.

Financial markets and long-term management

My fourth story has to do with currency and the management of the Charles Leopold Mayer Foundation's estate.

The Foundation, which aims to be involved in long-term actions, had also to project the management of its estate in the long term. Its founder had in fact made most of the fortune that he bequeathed to the Foundation by setting up international investment funds in the wake of the First World War. He was born in the 19th century and was profoundly immersed in the systems of thought of that period, Saint-Simonism in particular. He had faith in progress and faith in the development of exchanges and that is what led him to place most of his investments in transportation. But he did so in a very long-term perspective. Thus, for instance, he wagered on civil aviation in the early 1920s. This wager, which he maintained throughout the decades paying no regard to stock market fluctuations, however long they lasted, was one of the major sources of his prosperity. When we took over the Foundation about 20 years ago, we had to seek financial managers and at first we found only short-term managers, who were so steeped in the 'casino economy' that had developed since the deregulation of the financial markets, that they could not even imagine that there could be another way of reasoning. I then saw the absurdity of maintaining capital in pension funds, which, although they should have been mainly focused on the very long-term concern of providing pensions and more broadly, the prosperity of future generations, were using very short-term management tools. As a result, there was no financial vehicle adapted to guiding the very long-term mutations that were necessary for our survival.

The area of legitimacy of market mechanisms

My fifth and final story has to do with the conditions of legitimacy of the market economy.

For more than a century, ideological debates were dominated by the confrontation between liberal economics and Communism, between the advocates of a market economy and those of a public, planned economy. This ideological battle obviated a much more basic issue: why, and in what conditions can the market be technically legitimate? Allow me to explain: the market is one way of regulating exchanges among others, one particular form of governance. The conventionality of economic teaching has led us to forget this basic truth, which was very well-known by the moralists and philosophers from the Middles Ages to the 18th century, since the accumulation of material goods was considered at the time as a lesser evil and as a way of managing individual passions for them to be the least destructive to the community. Once you stop considering the law of supply and demand as a sort of universal law of gravity and instead see it as one form of governance of human societies among others, you have to submit it to the same questions that have to be asked about governance: in what conditions is it legitimate? One of the conditions for the legitimacy of governance is the 'principle of least constraint'; that is, governance is legitimate when in the name of the common good, it demands the fewest possible sacrifices of each individual citizen's freedom. Governance that imposes enormous restrictions on individual liberties and does not even suitably provide the common good will be judged sooner or later by the population as illegitimate, even if it takes a 'legal' form adopted as a result, for instance, of a democratic vote. When we apply this reasoning to the market to see how the rules of the market affect the different goods and services that are exchanged, then we discover that there is not just one type of goods and services, as claimed by total-market advocates who would like to pour everything into the same blender, and that neither are there just two types of goods and services; that is, market goods and public goods. My thinking led me to identify instead four types of goods and services:

- those that are destroyed when shared (which is the case for ecosystems and is the image of Salomon's judgement: when you cut a child in two there is no more child at all);
- those that are limited in quantity and are divided when shared, which is typically the case for natural resources, which require sophisticated mechanisms to reconstitute the resource, as well as mechanisms to share among all a wealth that belongs to all;
- those that are the main fruit of human genius and are developed indefinitely as genius itself develops;
- and finally those that are multiplied when shared, such as love, celebrations, social relations, knowledge, information, and so on.

According to this typology, the market is legitimate for the third category of goods but the goods belonging to the fourth category, which are multiplied when shared, are part of a different logic, which we call *mutualisation*.

In my view, the issues raised in these five stories constitute a vast work programme for foundations in the coming years and decades, a programme that would help develop the systems to ensure a 'right use of money'.

A work programme for foundations to cooperate on

In the 1980s, the Charles Leopold Mayer Foundation was the first in France to back projects of socially responsible savings, ethical investment, and micro credit. In 1987, for instance, it produced a film on the Grameen Bank, at a time when micro credit had not yet been swathed in the sort of magic virtue it was to be given later. In this film, we showed that micro credit was far from being a miraculous remedy; that it demanded discipline and social control (something that its advocates were perfectly aware of but was later swept under the rug by those who, after the pioneers, became the unconditional apostles of micro credit). Having helped to introduce socially responsible banking ideas in France, the Foundation then, in the early 1990s, sponsored a comparative study of the experiences of the different existing initiatives and the constitution of FINANSOL, the federation of socially responsible banks.

Research then suggested the need for further study of the financial markets, which led the Foundation to set up a financial observatory in Geneva.

We now think that the time has come to undertake a radical study on currency. Electronic tools now make it possible to compute in detail what goes into a product and what is exchanged. The historical reasons that led to the institution of the currency that we use today are amply obsolete. Well beyond the local exchange trading schemes (LETS) that have been developed in the past 20 years or so, other forms of currency are appearing, in Japan and in Germany for instance, at regional and national scales. Through them, we can see, in a future far closer than it seems, a system in which different types of currency coexist, each for different levels of exchange.

Foundations, beyond their possible commitment to ethical funds, should unite to take the initiative of developing much more serious information and evaluation systems on the social and environmental responsibilities of companies, and even of territories. Present-day ethical funds, despite their value as an awareness-raising tool, are all too often based on superficial evaluation systems of the responsibility of corporations, whose public relations pitches are given the same importance as the facts. To appreciate the social responsibility of corporations, we cannot be restricted to the reports that they issue. Evaluation should also be based on the points of view of employees, subcontractors, customers, the authorities of the territory in which they are established, and so on. This requires information systems that are not presently within the reach of an isolated ethical fund or an isolated foundation. An international alliance among foundations and pension funds would make decisive progress possible in this domain.

Moreover, foundations should depart from an approach that is all too often problem-specific and remedial. They should stop giving themselves a good conscience by 'doing good' but splendidly ignoring the cause and the root of the problems. In the present context of economic globalisation, and of interdependence among societies and between humankind and the biosphere, foundations constitute tools that are practically unique. Unique in that their independence and their possibility of acting in the long term make it possible for them to approach problems at a variety of levels and to commit themselves to patient and determined research on alternatives. Such alternatives are no longer to be searched for exclusively through specific projects. They are to be sought, as shown by my different stories, in the systems of thought themselves, and in the systems of governance.

A world society is emerging, but it is a society without common values and without regulatory institutions that relate to today's interdependencies. This is why the Charles Leopold Mayer Foundation has decided that its first priority for the period 2003–2010 is to contribute to the emergence of a community and to guide the necessary changes in governance, ethics, and development models. We hope that this programme and these priorities will mesh with the wishes and commitments of hundreds of other foundations.

4

Restoring the link between money, price signals and ethics

Jonathan Dale

After an earlier career teaching French at the University of St Andrews, Jonathan Dale was led to live and work in Ordsall, Salford, where he helps a group of tenants to manage their social housing. He was also a part-time project worker with Church Action on Poverty for several years. He is a member of the Religious Society of Friends (Quakers) and has acted as Clerk of Quaker Social Responsibility and Education. In 1996 he gave the annual Quaker Swarthmore Lecture, entitled 'Beyond the spirit of the age'. Since that time he has served on the Rediscovering Social Testimony Group and wrote the introductory sections to its final report, *Faith in action – Quaker social testimony*, which was published in 2000.

> When the Stranger says: 'what is the meaning of this city?
> Do you huddle close together because you love each other?'
> What will you answer? 'We all dwell together
> To make money from each other'? or 'This is a community'.
> (T.S. Eliot, chorus from *The rock*)

I am not an expert on the detail of any of the issues surrounding the right use of money. I am simply a Quaker who has reflected on some of them through the prism of the Quaker Testimonies. These are our convictions as to what is ultimately true about our life on earth, because, if you like, they come closest to reflecting our intimations of the nature of God. These Testimonies are nothing unless we practise them and, in doing so, experience afresh the deep reality they point to. They can be crudely summarised as

Testimonies to Peace, to Equality, to Simplicity, to Truth and Integrity and to the Earth; but they are experienced truths – not mere notions or theories. My own practice of them has taken me from a university career in St Andrews to working with a housing cooperative in inner-city Salford. Such a change gives insights into inequality: I have taken a 50% pay cut in the process and still been immeasurably better off than the people I work with. Here, going as a family even on a subsidised day trip to the seaside can be a big financial decision. The same economic gradient has become transparent in my moving house from the desirable leafy suburb of Didsbury to Ordsall, through the body language and utterances of estate agents, for whom such moves are as unnatural in our economic system as water flowing uphill. It is such experiences that lie behind the simple arguments that follow.

The bonds that money or trading relations create in our contemporary economic system are impersonal ones. However, community cannot be made real through such an abstract process in which the deepest moral dimensions of relationships are hidden. The right use of money, I believe, cannot be properly understood within such a framework. This is because morality, as the T.S. Eliot quotation suggests, is necessarily, at the deepest level, about community. Or, as Thomas Cullinan writes in *The passion of political love:* "The great surprise, at least to the modern mind, is that the most central reality of life is not after all an isolated and autonomous self, but communion" (1987, p 40). The economic system, however, is based precisely on the primacy of the autonomous self. Its reliance on abstract money relations distorts behaviour towards short-termism and self-interest. This is inevitable, as the central question tends ineluctably to become, if money is the universal mediator, 'Can I afford to?', rather than 'Would it be right to?'.

This mechanism is reinforced because the monetary value of goods in the shop scarcely begins to reflect the true social and environmental costs of their production and distribution (let alone their disposal) so that those costs are hidden from the purchaser in the transaction that s/he makes. Buying and selling constantly hide the real ethical issues that lie beneath the surface of the transaction. It is not hard to understand that the miraculous system that provides us with an ever-increasing purchasing power and, supposedly, standard of living, is the very system that is plundering our environment in so many destructive ways, leaving us also in a real sense poorer than we were. That is why, however unfashionable it may be, we need to return to the conviction expressed by the Quaker, Shipley Brayshaw, in his Swarthmore Lecture of 1932, 'Unemployment and plenty':

> Economic life must be brought into harmony with the eternal principles which underlie all right relationships.

A very good example of how the hidden nature of the costs of things undermines the basis for right relationships can be seen in our use of the car. The car is undoubtedly very convenient for taking us to where we want to go, at the turn of a key, in comfort and relative speed. That is all that many (perhaps most) people believe is involved. And, yet, some of the same people will curse the noise pollution that damages their quality of life. Others will lament the enormous damage to wildlife, through loss of habitat, or the deaths of animals, birds and insects in their thousands. The health of others may be affected by traffic pollution or from the motor vehicle's destruction of the possibility of safe walking and cycling opportunities, notably children's ability to walk or cycle safely to school. In addition, there are all the costs of pollution from the production of oil, its transportation and refining. It is true, of course, that some will be able to take the decision of whether to switch on the engine or not in the light of all the additional costs, which are not currently reflected in the price of petrol at the pump; but we need to recognise that most people will be helped by an economic signal. Such a signal would be a petrol price that reflects the real cost to the community of the car use that is being chosen. Otherwise, the price mechanism provides a false signal that car travel is all right, when we know it damages the quality of life for almost all of us.

One further example must suffice to make the point: you can buy beautiful hardwood garden furniture from many garden centres and other outlets. Hardly any of it is vouched for as deriving from sustainably managed forests. Much of it is almost certainly from illegal logging of virgin forests in the Far East. There may indeed be a short-term gain for the loggers and the purchaser, but at the cost of the loss of a virtually irreplaceable common asset, the virgin forest with all its myriad life forms, many of which are now threatened with extinction. That cost is nowhere factored in to the purchase. The purchase is impersonal, almost abstract, devoid of any real context. Devoid, that is to say, of any relationship of the purchaser to the effects of their purchase on those who live where it was produced, or on the wider world in general. It has, therefore, no human depth, being reduced to naked self-interested financial power. Such an experience of the so-called 'free' market is actually one of irresponsible decision making. A system built on the exercise of personal financial freedom without regard to the consequences for others is a system that is designed to use money wrongly.

These views of the amorality of the economic system fit in with other approaches to it. The economic system that has been operating for over 300 years has extraordinary powers of production, distribution and exchange. However, in the process, it fuels a competitiveness that is too often destructive. It increases rather than decreases inequality both within and between countries. Its powerful advertising arm encourages us to feel we need all sorts of things that are inessential. ("The global business of the future must constantly amaze the consumer. He doesn't know what he wants", as one Wall Street guru put it.) It is destroying the richness and beauty of the world. In other words, as a Quaker, it seems to me that it is destructive of our Testimonies and, therefore, in the end, damaging to our very ability to envisage a moral economy. Free trade may have seemed like a foundation of a moral system based upon equal relations between self-interested individuals, but we have come to see that it is desperately damaging. And that is so not only in its inability to include all the costs of its interventions, but, more fundamentally, because self-interest is an inadequate basis for any morality.

How, then, could the deeper morality underlying our purchasing decisions be brought into the light? And how to become part of a wider common practice? (Whether this would entail a thoroughly reformed version of the current economic system, or a fundamentally different one is not the issue here.)

One obvious thrust is to enlarge the concept of fair trade (although

I would not want to do anything to harm the development of fair trade in its current usage). Ultimately for trade to be truly fair, it needs to have all the costs it entails built into the transaction. A model in which all the advantages are taken by producer and consumer, leaving most of the costs to society hidden, is profoundly distorting and in a sense untruthful. It is neither fair nor truly free, in that society at large is forced to bear most of the costs. It is freedom defined as licence to do what the two parties to the contract wish, regardless of the wider social and community impact of their transaction. It would create fairer and, indeed, freer, transactions if we were to move resolutely to a taxation system, which built into the overall price of a product or service all the costs that it imposes on us.

For example those items where the packaging is most frequently thrown away – cans, plastic drink bottles, crisp bags and the like, could bear the cost of the street cleansing programme in their pricing. The cost of disposal (whether by recycling or landfill) of cars, white goods and the like, should be reflected in their cost. Where products or services create pollution and other damage to the natural environment, those costs should be reflected in their price. In the case of motoring, this could be in the purchase price, by mileage charging or by fuel duty, or, indeed, a combination of these. Similarly with air travel: air travel pays nothing like its true cost. Aviation fuel is still not taxed and the noise pollution and global warming effects of such travel are enormous. Holidays by air need to become vastly more expensive to reflect their true costs, as do foodstuffs air-freighted in. Such goods and services at present are being effectively subsidised by our descendants, as they will have to pay most of the costs. Moreover, unfairly, such costs may bear most heavily on present and future citizens of poorer countries who are the least responsible for them, adding a new dimension of unfairness to the system.

By putting forward the argument that the costs of goods and services should reflect their true social and environmental costs over time, it is not intended to suggest that this will by itself be enough to create a socially and environmentally responsible market place. The effects of particular increases or decreases in prices might well be considerable and some people might well decide not to pay the higher prices. That would be positive in itself. But the central issue is whether it would encourage people to make buying – and selling – acts of social responsibility. It should help but many other changes of approach will be necessary.

These approaches will have to include fundamental changes to the trading relations of rich and poor countries and to the international institutions that distort those relations in the interests of the wealthy and powerful. The UN, the World Trade Organisation (WTO) and the International Monetary Fund (IMF) should cease to serve largely the self-interest of the richest and most powerful countries. In particular, the shameful agricultural subsidies, which the EU and the US have insisted on preserving at the expense of small farmers in developing countries, must be removed. These bear a large measure of responsibility for the deepening global inequality that creates a glaringly unacceptable face of the so-called free market. They are a gross distortion of the free market and actively promote global inequality. Indeed, to reduce this catastrophic polarisation of rich and poor nations we might also recognise that the money created by sweeping speculation on the money markets is largely divorced from the real economy and yet can have catastrophic effects on it. Such speculation should be taxed internationally as Tobin suggested, with the funds raised ear-marked for sensitive, mostly small-scale development projects in the poorest countries.

Further measures would be needed to encourage a greater degree of equality at home as well as abroad. The existing structure of business governance, which represents the interests of managers and shareholders almost exclusively, should be transformed. We need a real stakeholder approach to the governance of business. Shareholders should be seen as only one party, with the work force and the wider community being the other two. Both of these should be represented on the boards and should have an important role in setting executive pay. It would help if such revamped remuneration boards had a duty laid on them to set a maximum differential between the highest and lowest paid employees of a firm.

Another strategic change would be to move away from the largely meaningless indicator of gross national product (GNP) (where an increase in crime and increased expenditure on security measures would count, absurdly, as increases in the GNP) to use instead a version of the Index of Sustainable Economic Welfare. This attempts to capture the relationship between production and the quality of life. A new road, which destroys 'sites of scientific interest' and blights with noise the living environments of thousands, would be represented more subtly by such an index than by the crude GNP. Once more, this would help shift the debate from 'How much money have I got in my pocket?' towards the much more subtle 'How well off are we in the things that really matter?' or 'Is my quality of life improving or deteriorating?'.

There are innumerable further measures that could be taken which would lead to money being used in the right way. I have only been able to outline a tiny handful. Issues around debt, housing policy and mortgages, the governance of pension funds, personal taxation and so on are also important. However, beyond the necessary changes in policies, institutions and systems, we need to remember that the deepest and most durable changes are those that make a deep impact on the ways in which individuals want to behave.

I was recently reflecting on the effects on my life of Salford Council's improved recycling scheme. I have long done a daily litter round on the estate as an expression of my commitment to improving the quality of life of the community. Until recently, most of the rubbish I picked up had to be thrown into the bin. But, now that we have a box scheme which takes glass and plastic bottles, cans and cardboard as well as paper, I find my work greatly increased by having to wash and dry the dirty bottles and cans, and so on. Those who throw the stuff away on the street, or even in the rubbish bin, are clearly off-loading the costs onto the community, mirroring the processes I have described in the real economy. I have to accept that part of my time and efforts should rightly be put into this sort of activity to limit the harm done to the world that sustains us – *without any financial reward*. The broader social challenge we face is to imagine and develop structures that promote the common good and, at the same time, encourage the development of a responsive community where many people realise that their abilities and talents have been gifted to them. Anyone who truly grasps this, will want to repay all that she or he owes to others for their own social development and that of society as a whole. And they are more likely to be satisfied with sufficiency than to demand excess.

Quaker industrialists in the early 20th century formed an important section of Britain's entrepreneurial class. There were enough of them to hold conferences just of Quaker industrialists. They had to face up to the critique of Friends (Quakers) of a radical political persuasion, who showed them that the economic system over which they presided was destructive of the Quaker Testimonies that supposedly were at the heart of all their actions. And, indeed, they and Friends generally were persuaded that the free market needed to be moralised by the state through all manner of socially organised measures of social welfare. In time the welfare state was duly created.

There is no equivalent body of Quaker industrialists today. Yet our times have something in common with the late 19th and early 20th centuries in that we also face a self-confident free market system, which is now promoting (at times with a disturbing triumphalism) what has become known as 'globalisation'. Once more, the safeguards, international this time, are not in place. There is little evidence of a global welfare state. In the face of an economic system in which differential rewards are creating increasingly polarised economic circumstances both nationally and internationally, there is abundant evidence that money is not rightly used to create decent conditions for all. Perhaps we need to see a more organised grouping of enlightened owners and managers who are open to the need to change course in such ways?

At the heart of a new approach to economics, we need to see self-interest displaced in favour of a much wider set of rights and obligations that prioritise meeting the basic needs of all. As Basil the Great wrote in the 4th century AD:

When a man strips another of his clothes, he is called a thief. Should not a man who has the power to clothe the naked but does not do so be called the same? The bread in your larder belongs to the hungry. The cloak in your wardrobe belongs to the naked. The shoes you allow to rot belong to the barefoot. The money in your vaults belongs to the destitute. You do injustice to every man you could help but do not.

Many will see such attitudes as unrealistic. However, Quakers have always believed that the Testimonies that guided their lives were for all. The experience of fulfilment in the furtherance of the common good is not inherently open only to a small minority but to everyone. Perhaps in the end it will be the philosophy of self-interest that will be shown to be unrealistic as it catastrophically fails to prevent the multiple environmental crises that are beginning to beset us. The right use of money will not be achieved without a rediscovery of our need to approach all the issues of resource creation and distribution through the prism of community.

References

Cullinan, T. (1987) *The passion of political love*, London: Sheed and Ward.
Tobin, J. (1978) 'A proposal for international monetary reform', *Eastern Economic Journal*, vol 4, pp 155-9.

5

Encouraging enterprise and decentralisation

Stephen O'Brien

Stephen O'Brien MP (Eddisburg, Cheshire), formerly Shadow
Paymaster General and Secretary to the Treasury, is currently the
Shadow Secretary of State for Industry. Born in Tanzania, he is Chair
of the all-party British Tanzania Group, Vice Chair of the all-party
Heavily-Indebted Poor Countries Group and of the all-party Uganda
Group, and an executive committee member of the all-party Africa
Group. Before becoming an MP in 1999, having first practised in the
City of London as a solicitor, for 10 years he was a senior executive
with international manufacturing industrialist, Redland plc (building
materials products), operating in 35 countries around the world, and
has also been engaged in a number of small businesses.

In this chapter I want to explore some of the ways in which
financial resources can be a force for good, not only in Britain
but also across the globe. This issue raises questions not only
about the best use of money but also about its generation – that is,
about how best to ensure that the resources are actually available to
be used wisely.

Often, governments that seek to create an enterprise climate, to
keep taxes down, to limit the role of the state, are accused of fostering
selfishness. Yet it is precisely such policies, at home and internationally,
which create the conditions in which more resources can be
generated.

That is as true internationally as it is in Britain. Trade is now the
most important factor in the fight against poverty in the developing
world. The level of inward direct investment produced by global
trade dwarfs levels of foreign direct assistance. The rapid spread of

globalisation has underpinned this trend, but has also (accompanied by the increasing role of digital technologies and transnational corporations, and the creation of the World Trade Organisation) presented developing countries with a complex and challenging trading regime.

It is vital that developing countries are allowed to realise the benefits for their populations that genuine trade liberalisation would bring. It has been estimated that successful implementation of the commitments made at Doha could add some $150 billion to the income of developing countries. The Conservative Party is fully behind the government in its efforts to achieve success in the Trade Rounds. We have also long called for reform of the EU's common agricultural policy, and for richer countries' agricultural markets to be opened up to others. Massive protection of European agriculture has for too long crowded out developing country producers. This has to change.

Of course, much more is required if real poverty is to be alleviated. Britain can be proud of its position as a leading advocate for developing countries and prouder still that we are prepared to act to back up our words. It is heartening and important, for example, that there is consensus in the House of Commons over such Millennium Development Goals (to be achieved by 2015) as halving the number of people living in extreme poverty from 1995 levels; universal primary education in all countries; and reducing maternal mortality by three quarters.

The work of the last Conservative administration in negotiating the Toronto Terms in 1988, the Trinidad Terms in 1991 and the Naples Terms in 1994 (which offered 67% debt relief on government-to-government debt) culminated in the Heavily-Indebted Poor Countries (HIPC) Initiative in 1996. This was the first comprehensive effort to eliminate unsustainable debt in the world's poorest, most heavily indebted countries.

The Labour Party has built on that record – that consensus – and their reforms of HIPC, providing more debt relief to more countries and faster, have made a real difference in reducing the burden of unsustainable debt and all that that burden entails, in terms of poverty, famine and disease.

As a result of the consensus-building exercise on HIPC, some

$100 billion of debt relief will be provided. Charities and faith groups – notably those involved with the Jubilee 2000 campaign and its successors – can also be proud of their involvement in building an increasingly international consensus.

We also welcomed the proposals developed by Gordon Brown and the then International Development Secretary, Clare Short, for an International Finance Facility that aims to increase the amount the developed world spends on aid as a means of achieving the Millennium Development Goals.

However, consensus will always have its limits. I do not believe that the present government is spending the international aid budget effectively enough. Nor is the EU. It would be better if more of that money were spent via non-governmental organisations (NGOs), including through charities with local knowledge, instead of through foreign governments with their own priorities. But clearly a formal liaison structure would be necessary; NGOs would have to have close liaison with foreign governments.

Much more focus is needed on aiding those countries with sustainable good governance: sound economic policies, effective institutions, the rule of law and democratic accountability. The quality of the aid is just as important as the quantity.

But the most important lesson of all is that aid itself is not enough. We have all seen the Oxfam adverts: 'Give a man a fish and he can feed himself for a day. But give a man the means to catch his own fish, and he can feed his family for years'. He could also sell some fish. Enterprise and trade are the keys to economic development, as I have seen for myself in countries as different from each other as Tanzania, where I was born, Kenya, where I was brought up, and in my membership of many all-party Parliamentary Groups for African and South American countries.

So the lesson that trade will ultimately be more effective than aid is a vital one. But this is part of a broader, still more fundamental, lesson from the history of the last century, in both developed and developing countries: namely the importance of free enterprise.

Just as all political parties recognise the need for aid to the developed world, so all realise that free enterprise has its limits. Considerations of equity, and of market imperfection, will always lead to government intervention – not least to help those whom the market economy alone might leave behind. There will always be a need for some state intervention in the economy.

However, the advantages of the market process should not be underestimated. These advantages relate both to the freedom it provides for people to express and satisfy their own requirements, and to the outcome this often produces in terms of increased efficiency, through the competitive dynamic and the provision of information about people's needs and wishes.

So there needs to be a compromise between free enterprise and government intervention. The question, of course, is the boundary between the two. It is a question facing developing and developed countries alike. And as the ongoing debate surrounding trade, 'globalisation' and their likely effects demonstrates, this is still very much a live question as policy makers worldwide consider the best response to the problems in the developing world.

Fortunately there is now plenty of empirical data that might lead us towards an answer. For the developed world has, itself, followed two rather different approaches over the last century. They might broadly be characterised as the American model of economic development and the continental-European model. Both have aimed to improve the prosperity of their peoples while maintaining an equitable outcome. And they have achieved rather different results.

Continental-European governments have chosen – deliberately – not to emulate the US model of free markets and low taxes, but rather implement the much more regulatory *dirigiste* or corporatist model. Their aim is laudable: protection for the most vulnerable in society. But the result of their approach has, more often than not, been quite the opposite.

The Organisation for Economic Co-operation and Development (OECD) publishes several indices of labour market flexibility that illustrate this point. They look, for example, at the strictness of labour market regulation, and the extent of non-wage labour costs. The US has a more liberal approach than Europe and, in almost every case, the UK is the most liberal in the EU itself. Furthermore the evidence since 1980 suggests that the gap between the EU and the US in terms both of unit labour costs and tax has widened further in the last two decades.

What has been the result of the European *dirigiste* model?

Ironically it is precisely those most vulnerable, weakest members of society – the very people who European governments sought to help with their regulatory agenda – who are hit first and worst when excessive government intervention inhibits job creation. This is especially important at times of global economic uncertainty.

Analysis of data on growth, unemployment and job creation shows just how poor Europe's record is, when compared with the US. Since 1980, GDP has risen by 61.1% in the EU, compared with 92.6% in the US. Meanwhile, total employment in the EU has risen by 27 million since 1980, but by 37 million in the US. The US has consistently had lower unemployment rates – with a EU average unemployment rate of 8.5% since 1980, even including times of economic growth.

Furthermore, Europe's unemployed stay jobless longer. An article in the US *Monthly Labor Review* (June 2002, p 20) calculated that, in the case of Europe's G7 members,

Almost half of Europe's unemployed remain jobless for a year or longer, while less than 10 percent fall into that category in the United States.... The proportion of long-term unemployment in Europe remains persistently high even during and after recoveries. In the United States, it is relatively low even during downturns in the economy.

The rate of growth of the labour force in the US has been phenomenal – over 50% higher than in Europe. Furthermore, investment in the US has been almost double that of European levels.

Last year, a British government White Paper looked at the implications of some of these figures. Had the EU's 64% employment rate been raised to the 75% rate of the US, the result would be 28 million extra jobs.

Of course, some of these trends may reflect the different lifestyle choices of the countries concerned. But overall the implications of the path that Europe has taken, compared with the US, is clear: lower incomes and fewer jobs. It is impossible to have a debate about the right use of money unless these fundamental lessons about the generation of money are learnt.

Furthermore there is one more lesson: it is during the periods of enterprise growth in Britain that charitable giving has risen and the voluntary sector expanded.

That is the other key theme I wish to explore: the role of the voluntary sector in ensuring that money is a force for good, and of government in fostering that sector. This does not, of course, diminish the need for government itself to use money wisely, for example in the alleviation of need and in the funding and some cases direct provision of important services. Indeed, my party has a package of reform proposals for the public services which we believe will foster the best use of taxpayers' money – often by giving more control to those who use the services. But the voluntary sector should also play an important part in any debate about the right use of money – both because a society with a thriving voluntary sector is a civilised society, and because in many cases the charitable sector is more flexible, more innovative and more people-focused than the services provided by Whitehall and Town Hall direction.

In considering social policy we would always do well, as our starting point, to remember Disraeli's words of 3 April 1872, that "in attempting to legislate upon social matters the great object is to be *practical* – to have before us some distinct aims and some distinct means by which they can be accomplished".

I know that moves to increase the involvement of the charitable sector in the public sector need to be handled with great care. Again, we recognise the fears that some in the sector have expressed that charities will replace public sector providers and donations will dry up. Government should work closely with the sector to ensure that wider roles do not mean slimmer cheques. And the voluntary sector should not replace public funding but add value to the public sector. There is a lot for national and local government to learn about *how* to spend, not just *how much* to spend.

Some will say that the problem is resources. But it is not about resources alone. There is a huge variation in performance between different local authorities. Indeed the Social Services Inspectorate reported last year that "People are fitted to services, rather than services to people". Charities and the voluntary sector, then, can teach us about fitting services to people. Government should value working with the charitable sector and learning from its experience and expertise. Of course, many have come to the same conclusion already, which is why the voluntary sector has been called upon to play a bigger role in the public services. But, I repeat, charities must not be used merely to prop up crumbling state structures. And neither should vulnerable people have to wait and hope for the failing state to find the right partners from the voluntary sector.

We want to help vulnerable people achieve dignity and this is best done by ensuring that they get help from those that understand their needs best. And very often that will be a voluntary group. It is vital that we establish a direct relationship between what people want and the support the voluntary sector gets from the public purse. At the same time, people must not believe that their obligations to neighbours in need begin and end with the payment of taxes.

Of course, any enhanced role for charities should not mean that the voluntary sector becomes just another branch office of central government, which I fear is the Labour Party's direction. The aim should be to unleash voluntary sector innovation, not issue directives from central command. We will actively resist any hint of the government's centralising tendency.

For us, the sector is part of the Conservative Party's vision for a new political settlement, one that stresses localism over centralisation, diversity over uniformity, and innovation over rigid, standardised, targeted control. A target-setting, auditing, performance-indicating approach has become a defining feature of the government's policies towards the public sector. And a large file of evidence proves that these targets are all too often forgotten, fudged or failed.

Too many voluntary groups fear becoming institutionalised in this bizarre arrangement, where setting a target is more important than achieving it. Thus, more and more time is spent setting targets and applying for grants and writing reports and formulating impact surveys – and less and less time is spent finding new ways of helping people!

The costs of red-tape risk excluding the smallest charities who are the most adept at the ethos of localism and often the most innovative in matching the needs of their community with the necessary course of action.

Certainly the government has a duty to account for the way it spends taxpayers' money. There will have to be certain minimum standards, but we believe there should be no straitjacket that all organisations must adhere to. Of course, past best practice will not be ditched simply in the name of modernisation.

The potential of the voluntary sector lies in what it *alone* can achieve. It is in the way that charity refreshes the parts that governments cannot reach.

If we are to add value to state services, we are going to have to trust people on the ground; trust charities and the voluntary sector to do their job, not headlock them into a wrestling match with contracts and departmental regulations in the name of 'partnership'.

In all these areas, it is right for government to appreciate its limitations – to appreciate that often others know best about the right use of money, whether voluntary groups or individual people themselves. And that often it is through governments getting off the backs of people and business that enterprise can flourish, and resources can be generated to spend wisely at home and to help replace the blight of poverty, famine and disease abroad with sustainable and increasing prosperity and real hope.

Part Three: Ethical dimensions

The chapters in this section are particularly concerned with the ethical dimensions of the 'right use of money'. Here, the authors suggest that individuals, companies and governments should be clear about their own moral and ethical stances; that is, on their own understanding of the right use of money. From this flow conclusions about how they might approach investment and the spending of resources.

For the use of money to have a moral dimension, **Tony Stoller** is concerned that monetary values reflect the true social costs of production and distribution. It needs to be less impersonal so that its link to relationships and interdependencies within communities is clearer. He suggests a number of approaches that would help move towards this.

Julia Neuberger emphasises the need to create a 'culture of giving' so that people are motivated to use money in altruistic ways. She suggests that it is the responsibility of all stakeholders in society to encourage this and suggests a number of measures that might contribute to a greater emphasis on 'giving' for the benefit of all.

From a Christian perspective, suggestions from a recent report of the **Church of England's Doctrine Commission** suggest that money no longer reflects productive activity, but is valued and speculated on in its own right, with the danger that it is idolised. The monetary system is seen as a force with power, rather than a utility that people are free to use as they wish. The 'right use of money' by individuals requires recognition that this force has to be managed by individuals, rather than meekly accepted.

Also at the individual level, **Charles Handy** points out that, above a certain threshold, more money does not necessarily lead to greater happiness. He suggests that individuals need to define what is 'enough' so that affluence ceases to be the sole symbol of success. Money can then be used for purposes other than increasing your own personal wealth. However, he does note that spending and hence pursuit of income allows the economy to grow, so that perhaps it is necessary for a more acquisitive approach to be maintained during the part of the lifecycle where career development and support of family is most important.

At the corporate level, **Philip Collins** argues that it is a retrograde step to rely solely on the 'business case' as a justification for corporate social responsibility. He believes that the moral case for corporations to be concerned about all their stakeholders – and not just shareholders – should be more explicit. This would involve a return to business ethics as a driving force and introducing a tradition of philanthropy back into corporate thinking about social responsibility.

At the state level, **Polly Toynbee** believes that there is a moral imperative for governments to ensure that enough of the country's wealth is used to support more vulnerable people in society, particularly those with low incomes. She suggests that an environment needs to be created in which the wage differential between the highest paid and the lowest paid return to pre-1980s levels, that the political case for ending low pay in the public services is made and that there is more redistributive taxation from the highest paid to the less well off.

6

Linking money and morality

Tony Stoller

Tony Stoller is a Quaker who has been active in the public sector as a
broadcasting regulator and in the commercial world as a senior
manager in both media and retailing. He works currently with the
new communications regulator, Ofcom. His 2001 Swarthmore
lecture and associated book, *Wrestling with the angel*, explored the role
of Quakers in commercial and public life.

I t is all too easy to feel that the modern world is characterised by
a wide, deep canyon separating money and morality. Some images
suggest that on either cliff edge, facing each other, stand the
preachers and apostles of either God or Mammon, each speaking
with the vehemence of utter conviction in language their antagonists
cannot understand.

Actually, that vision is not new. In the middle of the 16th century,
the medieval principles still held sway, and even as society changed
around them, and partly at least as a consequence of their actions,
there was, in Tawney's words, "a constant appeal from the new and
clamorous economic interests of the day to the traditional Christian
morality" (1926). A hundred years later all that had changed, and
by the middle of the 17th century, up to and including the modern
day, it was widely perceived that "the claim of religion to maintain
good rules of conscience in economic affairs finally vanished".

And that is not quite right either. Ever since the rise of a capital-
based society – driving and driven by the development and
exploitation of technology – money and morality have lived uneasily
together, not separated by a great divide, but sharing the same ground.

In many ways, that makes the discussion of the right uses of money
more difficult. It was easier in the brief ill-conceived certainties of

the 1980s when 'greed was good', to side with either the masters of the monetary universe or those who denounced them. The apparent separation, however, was unreal, as the subtleties of most other times show, including our own.

Each of us is at one and the same time a user of the economic, market, consumer society and the pilot of the morality guiding our own souls. If I shop for fruit, I am making an economic choice based on my appetite, my perception of value for money, and the wealth I can apply to that transaction. I am also making a moral decision about my acceptance of a world where fruit for sale is grown and harvested by people in the developing world who (at best) may scarcely benefit from that transaction; where goods are moved across the globe at considerable expense to natural resources; and so forth.

There are a few genuine ascetics, who can live a life largely devoid of monetary concerns. There are some for whom money is wholly sufficient. For the rest of us, the dilemma is constant.

It is a dilemma also for the corporate world. In keeping with our fondness for reducing the complex idea to a marketing slogan, it is now *de rigueur* for companies and institutions to adopt corporate social responsibility policies. That reflects an awareness among most of those who are responsible for organisations that their very business efficiency and prospects are damaged if they are seen to be operating in ways harmful to their environment or to society in their sourcing of supply, in their dealings with people and in their own commercial morality. For the more perceptive among them, there is an understanding that this is not just a necessary defensive posture. Running a corporate entity according to good principles of social responsibility will most likely help it to perform better. That was the experience of Quaker traders, whose reputation for good measure, for keeping their word in a bargain and for not selling adulterated goods, underpinned their considerable commercial success.

In this context, money is simply another commodity. It has no innate moral quality. That, however, depends on its use. The guiding principles here for consumers are that money should be deployed for necessities, for proper enhancements of life, for the help of others, but with a level of informed awareness that ensures it is not to be used in a way that damages other people, the environment, or indeed the individual themselves. For corporate entities, money is well spent if it is properly and proportionately acquired, deployed in a decent manner for the (decent) ends of the organisation, fully and openly accounted for, and provides fair profit without the unreasonable enrichment of those involved.

For those who are dealing with money in a more absolute sense, much the same principles are going to apply. For the individual, there is a personal expectation that acquiring wealth, giving charity, and helping others in need is done in line with a personal morality at least. For institutions charged with more substantial charitable and social enterprise, there will always be a requirement for clear principles, soundly based in both intellect and practice, which are fully transparent and against which they are regularly held to account. If they are giving money to other groups of individuals, they will seek equivalent standards of intention, practice and reporting from those who receive.

One of the key figures in Quaker history, John Woolman, emphasised that the use of money must accord with the individual's responsibilities for deploying something entrusted to them for the common good.

All we possess are the gifts of God. Now in distributing it to others we act as his steward. If the steward ... takes that with which he is entrusted and bestows it too lavishly on some, to the injury of others ... he disunites himself and becomes unworthy of the office.
(Woolman, 1763)

It is not for nothing that the first ethical investment fund carries the significant title of *Stewardship*. The question that follows is how to determine what are those underlying principles of trust, and how they can be sustained.

It would be facile to argue that one or other set of ethical or religious principles are the only way to ensure that the steward carries out his task faithfully. But I can assert with confidence that good practice arises from a deep grounding in one or other coherent codex. Those will have developed organically over a period of time, with broad input of both intellectual and probably religious perception. They will apply across the wide range of human experience, being not just ways of managing money, but sets of principles against which to live your life, and by which to guide and govern a society.

For example, I have no doubt that the successes of Friends Provident were rooted in that company's Quaker origins, not because Quakerism is good or bad at money management or life insurance or investment, but because the Quaker way of living as a whole provides a sound base for both the individual and the world view. Not the only valid one, to be sure, but one tested and validated over time. 'Stewardship' itself grew out of this, bringing a moral dimension into practical financial management. It was and is guided by the belief that not only do we need to conduct our investments with every effort to avoid doing harm, but that we can actually seek positively and confidently to make them a force for good in our society.

To ensure a proper use of money, therefore, we need reassurance that claims to virtue are real, and not merely cosmetic. From a Quaker perspective some look with scepticism at some of the claims made by self-styled 'ethical investments', and some of the lists of companies where investors are being told that they can place their money, confident that it is being invested according to good principles of corporate social responsibility. That is the catch with the widespread homage being paid to corporate social responsibility (CSR). How can we tell whether or not, in particular instances, it has substance or is merely another example of the culture of 'spin'?

The answer lies in the availability of sound information to back up such assertions. The concept of CSR has also to deliver on transparency and accountability. Thus, judgements about the proper use of money in the sense of investment cannot concern themselves only with the apparent rectitude of the product or service in question. They must also be based upon the ready availability of evidence of good practice. The same will apply in the allocation of charitable funds. Is the recipient organisation well run, and open to enquiry to demonstrate that? On that basis and on that basis alone can we be confident that our donations or support are being well applied.

The other guarantor is the ethical and/or religious grounding that I have argued is essential for organisations that pursue broader social or charitable aims, or for those companies and enterprises that rely on such a base. To be confident that their application of finance, or our allocation of money to them, is sound, we will need to be sure that they are not afflicted by what we may speak of as 'ethical creep'. Slippage away from what might be entirely genuine starting principles is all too easy. To guard against that, such a social enterprise needs to retain its links with the tradition from which it has arisen. That is not always the best commercial decision, in the sense of managing short-term issues, nor always the most convenient in administrative or political terms. In the medium term, however, it will be seen to be by far the best way. There is at work here an example of enlightened self-interest, whereby staying in touch with the roots can sustain the prospects of an undertaking far better than the pursuit of immediate advantage involving abandoning such underlying principles.

In the modern world, money and morality are intricately entwined. Judging the rightness of use depends upon full access to information and proper accountability. Where we are asked to have confidence in an enterprise because of its ethical or religious roots, we need to be satisfied that the undertaking will keep faith with those roots, and remain grounded in the principles which go beyond the merely commercial. The Quaker experience is one example of how remarkably beneficial such a practical philosophy can be, both for the enterprises themselves and for the society in which they operate.

References

Stoller, T. (2001) *Wrestling with the angel*, London: Quaker Books.

Tawney, R.H. (1926) *Religion and the rise of capitalism* (Pelican Books edn, 1938).

Woolman, J. (1763) *A plea for the poor*, cited in (1995) *Quaker faith and practice*, London: Religious Society of Friends.

7

Encouraging a 'giving' culture

Julia Neuberger

Rabbi Julia Neuberger is former chief executive of the King's Fund (1997-2004), a former member of the Committee on Standards in Public Life (2001-4) and a trustee of the Booker Foundation. She was awarded a DBE in the 2004 New Year's Honours and created a life peer in June 2004.

> Money makes the world go around.
> Money, money, money, money.... (*Cabaret*)

Seen as the source of all ills (greed for it), or as the enabler of all good things (many economists and charitable fund raisers), money is seen as dirty, not to be talked about, essential, the focus of most political debate.

In fact, money – as a resource – is neutral, ethically speaking. How it is acquired, how it is spent, and what purposes it is used for are the questions with a moral overtone. And wider society should welcome the Friends Provident Foundation's desire to have a wide-ranging, far reaching debate.

For me, there are three key points:

- the duty to make life fairer;
- ensuring that money is given well, not badly;
- and the need to create a culture that encourages people to use their money for social good.

Making life fairer

First, life is unfair. But we have, as individuals and as society, a duty to attempt to make it fairer. In Jewish terms, this means the giving of *tsedakah*, usually translated as charity, but in fact meaning 'social justice'. All of us are obliged to give 10% of our income or our wealth.

From this idea comes the idea of tithing. But central to the Jewish thinking in this area is that we are not doing anything particularly virtuous by giving 10%. The real charity (over and above duty) is giving upwards of 20%, and time, energy, devotion, love. Those deeds are called deeds of loving kindness, and are of a different order. Even if money is involved, it is likely that it is not money alone.

So all of us have a duty to give. That idea of evening up by individual giving, leading ultimately to the use of progressive taxation as a way of society evening up a bit, is widely accepted. Money from rich to poor, from fortunate to unfortunate, from old to young or young to old. Transfer of assets for social good is something most of us approve of to some extent, as long as it does not impinge too much on what we want to do.

However, there is another concern that affects this need to give: that of having too much money, life too easy. And we need a debate on how wealthy and middle-class parents make their children's lives too easy, with children who do not need to work, who rely on parental handouts, who are not self-sufficient. The need to earn money is an important driver in creating entrepreneurial thinking. Creativity needs a bit of urgency, a bit of a driver.

And the use of financial levers to 'incentivise' people has some virtues, as long as we realise people are driven by other rewards as well: recognition, self-fulfilment, a sense of altruism, opportunities for education and development. However, money – financial incentives – has its place. And those who have enough and have earned enough can then give more away.

Giving money well

The second key point is that giving money, as individuals and as societies or charitable foundations, is not easy. Giving badly leads to perverse consequences. Giving well, and often giving with others or in a particular way, can lead to gaining real change. In charitable foundation terms, although the spend is a mere speck when compared with government spending, a major grant can be used to shift an agenda. Wise use of money, therefore, can lead to profound change.

Examples abound, such as the Victorian philanthropists' spending on social housing, leading to a completely different way of thinking about the obligation to house the poor. Or, in modern terms, charitable giving (Rowntree, for instance) can lead to new thinking about elderly people, or in our case (the King's Fund with the Sainsbury Centre for Mental Health) to demonstrating the value of new ways of engaging with people with severe mental illness, in this case a process known as assertive outreach.

So, money can relieve poverty and it can – when well spent and well considered – effect social change. It can improve education, alleviate hunger, change perceptions of particular groups and, in the hands of charities, do the 'soft' improvements that governments are not sure about and cannot demonstrate the need for. This can be about art or the environment, about music and culture, or even – before obesity began to be the fashionable cause – sport and sporting facilities. In all these causes, money can be used for good. And usually is.

Encouraging a giving culture

The third key point is about encouraging people to use their money for social good. Government has tried to make the giving of charitable contributions more attractive in tax terms. It is changing the definition of charity via a public benefit test. Those on higher tax rates get a real tax break from giving. But this is not enough. And it is not part of the culture. The young give less than the old. The Northern Irish give more than the rest of the UK per capita.

What needs to be done to create a giving culture is far beyond what we have so far. Three approaches would contribute to this:

1. We should see all employees/educational institutions encouraging giving of money and time as part of their role in society – corporate citizenship on one level, but educators and encouragers of the younger workforce on another.

2. Second, a small amount of our income tax should be earmarked as 'charitable', for us to decide what area of public benefit we want it to go to, with a plethora of charities on offer as possible recipients. Like payroll giving, this would be automated. Unlike payroll giving, it would be part of tax, but it would be billed as being part of a social endeavour and it could also encourage people to think about where they would like their money to go.

3. Third, young people should be encouraged to do some kind of public service (a bit like national service, but community and environmental volunteering instead). As a thank you for, say, six months of working in a hostel or on canal regeneration, they should be rewarded with money – not for themselves, probably, as that destroys the voluntarism – but as a small pot of cash they can give away. This would be part of creating a giving culture, far more powerful than the rather useless exhortations by government ministers.

None of these ideas is difficult. None is beyond the wit of man or woman. Yet creating a giving culture leading to a form of social harmony, with its own personal and institutional incentives within it, has never been more vital. This debate has only just begun, and government has been nervous of real innovation. This is the moment for charitable foundations, once real engines of social change, to make a difference to this debate – and to help raise the profile of the benefit of giving, as their founders once recognised.

8

Managing the power of money

Church of England Doctrine Commission

Stephen Sykes, Chair of the Church of England Doctrine Commission, has selected extracts from a chapter of the Commission's report *Being human: A Christian understanding of personhood, illustrated with reference to power, money, sex and time*, from the Church of England Doctrine Commission.

The Doctrine Commission of the General Synod of the Church of England advises the House of Bishops on Doctrinal questions referred to it by that House. Its membership is drawn from theologians in universities, theological colleges and dioceses. It is chaired by the Right Reverend Professor Stephen Sykes, Principal of St Johns College, University of Durham.

What is money? The answer to this question appears obvious: notes and coins are, of course, money. But pointing to these objects would be a quite inadequate answer to the question. 'Money' is much more like a verb than a noun. Money is dynamic; it is activity; it is function.

What makes notes and coins money are the functions they perform in human society. For the notes and coins (and the figures on the accounts) to function as money requires a set of social, cultural and political, as well as economic, arrangements. Money is a human and social reality, not something that can be abstracted from specific human contexts. The nature and function of money are not constant but change through time and with social, cultural, economic and societal contexts.

One reason why it is not possible simply to 'read off' what the Bible says about money and apply it to our own situation is that money differs markedly in its nature and function between biblical times and our own day. Indeed, part of that difference lies in how very much less significant money was to economic life then. In those days there simply was much less money in circulation. The result was not merely that society was relatively less wealthy; rather, money did not perform the central role in economic life that it does in our society. Other means of exchange were more frequently used and wealth or poverty were related primarily not to possession of money, but of land. By contrast, in our case there are few aspects of modern life that are imaginable, much less navigable without it.

The relatively recent but extraordinarily far-reaching changes in the nature and function of money make it even more important to avoid abstraction and the suggestion that money is a simple, straightforward and unequivocal term and reality. It is these developments that also make it necessary to focus clearly on money in this discussion rather than wealth. For unless we recognise that recent developments in the system of money place us in a new situation, we shall either approach it in a superficial way with little theological reflection, or we shall apply outdated modes of analysis.

In its origin, money bore a fairly direct relation to the realities of human productivity and trade. Generally restricted in use to a specific community, it could perform a unitary function for that community in its producing and trading of goods and services. (Of course, money has been used to oppress and to serve selfish ends that work against the flourishing of the whole community; we are not reading that history through rose-tinted spectacles.) But with the break of the link between money and real wealth production, with the instruments of credit creation (that is, the instrument through which money may be increased vastly beyond the level of deposits held), globalisation and the technology permitting the transfer of money at the speed of light, the conditions were met for the creation of a market for instant trade in money as a commodity itself.

Both the fact and the actual working of the market in money have changed the nature of money. In excess of 90% of the worth of transactions do not relate to productivity in the real world at all, but represent speculations about the future value of a specific currency. Money almost entirely freed from a relationship to the value of goods and services in the lives of human beings and their communities has, in effect, been removed from the sphere of human values. Its growth and movement seek the optimisation, not of the conditions for human flourishing (or even of wealth creation through production, provision of services or trade), but of its own power to reproduce more of itself. The market in money follows its own laws, oriented on increasing the monetary value of investors' holdings of money – as though money were not only the arbiter of the worth of everything else, but a good and an end in itself, self-validating and self-legitimating. Money has taken on a life of its own.

While the relationship to the external realities of economic activity in the economy has been broken in one direction (from production and trade to currency: the backing of currency), it remains strong in the other. Confidence in the currency may be entirely unrelated to the worth of what is being conducted within it, but the speculative decisions made on the basis of such confidence (and the perceptions of others' future confidence and the decisions they will make) can and do determine the 'value' of one currency against another in ways that severely impact on the real world economy and the human beings that live within it.

Since more money is chasing goods and services, and because money is in principle insatiable in its demands, an economy and culture centred on money is prone to anxiety. Money will never arrive at a point where it is capable of being sated, of saying 'enough'. While the expansion of credit means that money no longer symbolises and represents stored wealth, it represents nonetheless a stored potential claim against the world's resources. And because the supply of money is ever expanding, these claims and the monetary power to pursue them likewise expand and consequentially distort markets based in some more direct relationship to human need or sufficiency.

We think of money as notes and coins, as a tool, or else as a possible object of desire among others that we may *freely* choose to pursue or not. The desires we fulfil through use of money, and even our love of and desire for money itself, are expressive of our spirit and its fundamental orientations in the world.

But are we right to assume that our spirit and its desires are self-constituting, shaped in some neutral sphere, expressive of a self and its desires already shaped and constituted apart from its relationship to money? Are we right to assume that we are free in relation to money, free to choose whether and how we associate our lives with it and what meaning it shall have for us? Are we right to assume that money is more like a substance (a tool or an object) than a field of force, an activity or a network of relationships? Are we right and is it safe to assume that money exerts no power? Are we right to assume that we use money instrumentally, to meet our needs and desires, without money itself shaping our needs and desires, our sense of what is good, right and true? Above all, are we right to assume that the kind of problem that money can be is fundamentally a personal one, a matter of our private, internal, moral or spiritual values and orientation? Moreover, are we right to treat these as uninvolved with and unshaped by the social dynamics and structures (including financial and economic ones) within which we live? Are problems with money, in essence, simply those of individual moral and spiritual failures, which express already-established pathologies of the self?

The assumptions behind these questions might be unsafe. Is there, after all something about our involvement with money that is less like possession or use of an object and more like a highly charged spiritual dynamic or force? That our use of money does not only give rise to issues that can be adequately handled through the (secularised?) language of ethics, but is a significant spiritual and theological issue? It would then not only be a matter for individuals of regulating their external behaviour, but of securing justice.

Especially in the Old Testament, considerations of the pathologies of money (gross poverty, unequal distribution of wealth, injustice, and so on) do not concern themselves exclusively with questions of individual decision making. Rather, questions of personal morality and spirituality are addressed in the context of broader socially institutionalised economic arrangements in which money has some kind of power. These suggest that money does not only have power over us when we freely choose to relate to it in specific ways that reflect some individual personal pathology on our part. Money also has power by virtue of what it is and how it functions in the order of a particular society – power for good, but also power for ill.

A belief in our inner freedom to mould our own desires about money, tempting though it is, is also challenged in our own experience. Can anyone believe that the increased availability of credit does not at the same time change our moral sense about whether it is good or bad to be in debt? Does not the frequency with which we see huge prizes awarded as the random outcome of a gamble and huge rewards given to those at the head of organisations (even failing ones) affect how far money starts to glitter before us, enticing us with its capacity to procure what we want and calm our fears of finding ourselves destitute and in need? These are rhetorical questions; the evidence of those we know, let alone the evidence of research into such topics as student indebtedness, gives a very clear answer: the human will is shaped by that with which human beings occupy themselves every day and the assumptions they find themselves making.

We have described money as a good, but also one that has acquired dominance in the lives of individuals and societies, and indeed on a global scale. The emergence of a human artefact such as money as something exercising a capacity to share, and even to dominate, human living is something Christians regard as entirely familiar. It is the phenomenon of idolatry. A fundamentally ingenious, creative, productive invention becomes that to which there is no alternative, a force commanding fear and even a sort of obedience. Is there a risk that money might be God's rival for the right to shape human lives?

Let us examine some of the ingenious inventions in which money plays a key part and discern its tendency to become more than a human creation. Insurance, for example, is in its origin a way in which human beings pool money in order to share a risk: we all pay a certain amount to insure against flooding, in order that the proportion who experience floods may not have to bear the whole burden of the disaster when it strikes. Similarly, we can share the risk of untimely or accidental death, or of motor accidents. But what happens when this invention comes to be seen (and of course profitably promoted) as a universal protection against risk, as something that can be offered as protection against almost anything? Have we not then come to change insurance from being protection against shared risks, precisely measured by statistics, into something quite different, the fantasy of a risk-free life? From a prudent invention, insurance is in danger of becoming something to be worn against danger.

Or what is happening when the game of placing small stakes on a chance outcome in a raffle, something that can be an amusing and enjoyable way of raising small amounts of money for a church or a charity, becomes through assiduous promotion a huge business venture on which, then, all sorts of society's requirements come to depend. Is not then a harmless piece of human playfulness emerging into a source of dependence as well as, in the case of some of the poorest people, offering a fantasy way out of poverty into riches instead of what they actually require, the means of having enough and being freed of worry about the basics of life? Or what are we to say when the prudent instinct to make provision for the care of elderly persons is so played on that we are enticed into more and more elaborate means of saving money, as though money will comfort our later years? We have already mentioned what happens to the benign institution of lending money when it is so promoted as to seem a necessary adjunct of life, and all our tomorrows are mortgaged and our freedom of manoeuvre sacrificed so that we can have today what otherwise might have had to wait until tomorrow?

As we go through these phenomena that illustrate the emergence of a human invention into the status of a controlling force in our lives (and many more examples could be given), we come face-to-face with the words of Christ:

No one can serve two masters; for a slave will either hate the one and love the other, or be devoted to the one and despise the other. You cannot serve God and wealth (Mammon). (Matthew 6.24)

Here money is given the name of a divinity as we are warned against the idolatry of money.

What being human before God means at the very least is the recognition that we are precisely 'human': of the ground, destined to be returned to it, earth to earth, ashes to ashes, dust to dust. This requires to be recognised in every aspect of living; but in relation to money it has a particularly poignant relevance. In common parlance it is money that is being referred to when it is said, "You can't take it with you", or, in the more sombre and profoundly accurate biblical words spoken at funerals (no doubt in the presence of executors and inheritors), "We brought nothing into this world, and it is certain we can carry nothing out" (cf 1 Timothy 6.7). The contemplation of the sharp reality of dying relocates our confidence from the money we have amassed to the God who freely gives new life to the dead.

Christians have always been encouraged to show prudence and foresight, as part of their preparation for death, in disposing of their money (and other wealth) by means of a will, so as to relieve those who come after them of undue worry and anxiety. However, the elaboration of techniques for tax-efficient maximising of one's estate can go far beyond prudence and foresight, and express instead a very different motivation.

The practice of the Christian life affords ample opportunity for those activities and contemplations that have the capacity to dethrone money and place us before God, with our money as human beings. The eucharistic meal with its echoes both of the free lunch for 5,000 described in the gospels and the free gift of release and redemption places us squarely before the central Christian paradox of grace, that what is free most certainly is not cheap. That is, the experience of being fed without cost is to draw us into a self-offering without conditions. Before God are set the gifts of creation and the product of human labour at the same time as the assertion is made that we have these things only through God's goodness.

Likewise, in the face of the generosity of God, it is generosity we seek to practice (in the sense both of carrying it out and of constantly rehearsing it) through the generous giving of alms, and it must be said, the joining in solidarity with the poor close at hand and far away in campaigning for justice, although it may (and especially when it will) cost us. In the act of generosity, we rehearse a dethroning of money as that on which we are tempted to rely for the protection and nourishment, which come from God.

Reference

Church of England Doctrine Commission (2003) *Being human: A Christian understanding of personhood*, London: Church House Publishing.

Acknowledgement

This extract, from *Being human*, is © The Archbishops' Council 2003 and is reproduced by permission.

9

Money: what is it for?

Charles Handy

Charles Handy is a writer and broadcaster. He has been an oil
executive, an economist, a professor at the London Business School
and the Warden of St George's House in Windsor Castle. His books
on the future of work life and organisations include *The hungry spirit*
and, most recently, *The elephant and the flea.*

Browsing through yesterday's business section of the paper, I
noted that a couple of our home-grown oil barons had each
taken home over £4 million in pay last year. And that's just
Britain! In America they would make ten times as much. What do
they do with it all, I wondered? Why do they need it? And is it fair
that they should get so much more than the people who work
with them? Or people like doctors and teachers and the police
who do equally valuable work? Then I caught myself speculating,
'What would I myself do with all that stuff?'. There was a touch of
envy there, mixed with dreams of riches. We are few of us immune.
Such a complicated thing it is, this money, I thought to myself, so
necessary and yet so intrusive, distorting our values and priorities.
Is it good or is it bad?

One thing is sure: we could not live without it. Money really
does make the world go round. Whether we are talking about a
country town, a country or the world, the mechanism that provides
us with work and food and fun – the economy – is no more than
an elaborate arrangement of barter systems, with money as the oil
that keeps it working. Come to think of it, if the barter currency
really were oil, we might not be so keen to pile it up. Where would
we keep four million barrels of the stuff? Part of the genius behind
the idea of money is its convenience. We can store it, measure it or

move it nowadays with a click on a computer keyboard. Something like 30 times the national income of this country flows through the City of London every day, and quite a few people earn their living by extracting tiny bits of it as it goes by. As many have discovered down the ages, it is often easier and more profitable to make money out of money than by actually producing something real. They used to call that usury. Now it is termed trading in derivatives and it is smart.

Yes, money is essential for life as we know it, but money also has acquired a life and a meaning of its own. For some, money on its own is a symbol of success. Those oil barons will almost certainly never get around to spending all that money. They do not have the time and they may well not have the inclination to go out and buy house, yachts or old paintings. Warren Buffet, the world's second richest man, after Bill Gates, lives simply, spends little. His wealth is just a measure of his business acumen. Others, whose wealth is not published in the papers, can use the money they make but do not need to buy some of those symbols of success. It might, I sometimes think, be simpler to take out an advertisement in those papers.

For others, money is often rightly termed compensation. I once invited the managers of an international investment bank and the head of a theatre company to describe their organisations to a conference of managers. Their products were obviously very different but the way the two organisations were structured and managed was remarkably similar, apart from the fact that the bankers were paid 20 times more than the actors. For the bankers, their work was a well-paid job, for the actors it was a calling. Lucky those whose calling is also richly rewarded financially, but for many money is the alternative to a vocation. It is not clear, then, who should envy whom. Is it better to be poor but doing what you believe in, or a rich prisoner in someone else's organisation?

Most of us, however, do not have that choice. We do what we do and a little more money would be nice, thank you. 'It's the economy, stupid', goes every politician's mantra, in the belief that more money will make everyone happier. Except that it seems that it does not. The research on happiness has a remarkable consistency across societies. It seems that where the average income in a society is under $10,000 a year, then more money does result in more happiness, as recorded by answers to standard questionnaires. Above that level, however, more money does not increase the average levels of recorded happiness. We are talking averages here, across total populations, so we should probably more than double that figure to find the happiness threshold for the average salary earner, but the stark fact remains that above a certain level more money does not make us happier.

Economists, however, would point out that it is important that we continue to believe that more does mean happier, because unless more people keep on spending more money our economies will not grow, there will be less to spend on public services and there will be less work and money for the poorer workers, including those in the developing world. It is, you might say, our social duty to spend more than we need to. Odd.

Such a complicated thing, then, is money. It is our livelihood, the way we pay for our bread and butter. It is the way we create work for other people. It is a product in its own right, in that you can make money out of money. It is a measure of success, whether you store it in a bank or spend it on unnecessary things. It is a consolation prize for missing out on your vocation. It can even be an excuse for not following that vocation, as when someone says 'Once I have made a million, I will be free to do what I really want to do'. No wonder that we get confused. No wonder that so many make money the point of life rather than the means of life. It was not meant to be that way when it was first devised as the universal mechanism of exchange.

At a personal level, life would be simpler if we followed the doctrine of 'enough'. This doctrine holds that unless and until we can define what 'enough' is for us in terms of money we will never be truly free; free, that is, to define our real purpose in life. You will, instead, be a volunteer slave to your employer or profession, subordinate to the priorities of others.

Settling for 'enough' does, however, mean that we have to do away with the other uses of money. It will no longer work as a symbol of success, or as a way of defining ourselves, or as an excuse or compensation for not getting on with our real life. We have to become open and honest about what we really value, about how we wish to define ourselves and how we want others to view us.

Having tried it, I can vouch for the fact that the honesty it requires of one is refreshing, even if it surprises and disturbs some of our friends who hope that it is not the start of some sort of fashion.

'Would that it were!', I often feel. The world would be a more varied and honest place. But then I come up against the economists who worry about the demand curve that creates the supply that translates into jobs and taxes. My compromise is to urge the doctrine of 'enough' on those of us in the Third Age, those who have passed beyond the stages of career and family. That is because it gets easier to work out what is enough as one gets older, when there is less need to provide for the uncertainties of the future and while there is still time to do what we feel we are on this earth to do. At that stage, too, our drop in consumption and earnings will not be significant enough to impoverish the third world. Our example might be one small strike against the tyranny of money in the modern world. It might give some hope to those who feel that there is no escape from that tyranny. It might even challenge the economists to find a way to break out from the often-vicious circles that money creates.

10

Returning business ethics and philanthropy to corporate social responsibility

Philip Collins

Philip Collins is Director of the Social Market Foundation (SMF), an independent think tank. He is the author of two novels and, before joining the SMF, was an equity strategist in two investment banks.

There is a great deal of argument at the moment about the idea of corporate social responsibility (CSR). It is an important idea. The question of how money is made and how it is deployed is a crucial one. The idea has been brought into the headlines by a now familiar litany of cases: the use of sweatshop labour by Nike and Gap in Indonesia and Cambodia; the problems encountered by BP in Colombia; Nestle's aggressive marketing of baby milk in developing countries; Shell's Brent Spa oil platform in Nigeria, and Monsanto's problems with GM soya beans.

Now, the argument has moved into a new phase. The attention of campaigners has shifted from the process by which profit is made to the very product itself. The best example of this is the case against the tobacco companies and the incipient argument against junk food. These campaigns deploy a mixture of health and moral arguments, although the former usually cloak the latter. One of the components of this new set of campaigns is the demand that companies act responsibly, as the drinks industry did in funding drink-driving campaigns and as the tobacco industry did not in denying into the last ditch that there was any link between smoking and lung cancer.

These cases all have one of two characteristics. Where they involve explicit law-breaking there really is nothing further to be said. The task for government is then simply to enforce the law and punish the wrongdoers. Companies are obviously not outside the law. They exist purely through licence. They are the beneficiaries of generous laws of limited liability through incorporation and they, of course, have a duty to obey the law, as we all do. The concept of CSR is simply redundant in these cases. It is superseded and entirely enclosed by the law. This shows us that a complete separation of companies from the instruments of the state has never been plausible. The classical economists, Adam Smith, Ricardo, Mill, all thought of themselves as engaged in a discipline called *political* economy in which all economic decisions had political links. The separation of economics and politics has been a great loss to both subjects.

However, unfortunately, most of the instances of CSR with which I began this piece are not straightforward. They are, instead, instances where Western companies are conducting businesses in countries where the rule of law is either weak or, sometimes, absent altogether. In many countries, bribery and corruption are redefined as normal business practice. In cases such as this, an appeal to the rule of law is not enough. It is precisely the weakness of the rule of law that is the problem and, in these instances a company needs to refer back to its own business ethics. CSR is meaningful in these cases, although it is little more than a re-labelling of the older discipline of business ethics. It is strange that the new entourage of CSR should have grown up with virtually no reference to (indeed in ignorance of) the reputable and useful literature of business ethics.

So far, so good. CSR, however, has come to mean a great deal more than appropriate ethical responses to difficult overseas dilemmas. In the six years since the first-ever minister for the subject was appointed, a great deal of ink has been spilled in trying to sharpen the definition of the terms. Unfortunately, the opposite has happened and every contributor to the conversation adds a new concern to the rubric of CSR. There is no better example than the Department for Trade and Industry's own website, which offers the following set of empty platitudes in search of a definition of CSR:

> ... to help promote the business case and celebrate business
> achievements, support partnership and business participation in key
> priorities including through co-funding, fiscal incentives and brokering
> new partnerships, ensure government business services provide helpful
> advice and signpost other resources, encourage consensus on UK and
> international codes of practice, promote effective frameworks for
> reporting and product labelling.

When everything is included, nothing is said. It is hard to get anything at all from this jumble of conflicting ideas. This would not matter if a great deal of money were not being spent, if every major company were not employing a consultant and if important issues were not being lost in the confused chatter. However, something important is being lost. I want to make the case for a clear CSR, comprised of two things: reputable business ethics and philanthropy.

What corporate social responsibility has become but ought not to be

A false prospectus of CSR has developed. Of what is it comprised? The term can refer, depending on the author or the company, to the way a company spends its money; how it makes it in the first place; how *much* it makes; the nature of its product; how and to what extent it remunerates its senior executives; how it reacts to a whole range of social, ethical and environmental risks; how it treats its employees; the company's investment in its community; its social and ethical policy development; the way it involves its employees in decision making; socially responsible investment; cause-related marketing; partnerships with charities; its control over the supply chain; environmental management; and social and environmental reporting.

Some of these questions are entirely legitimate. Of course, a company ought to be held to account for how it treats its employees. It is an extremely hard thing to police but, of course, it matters. In most markets, companies that treat employees badly will not keep their staff, but, at the lower end of the income scale in particular, this assumption would be very complacent indeed. That is precisely why there is elaborate and extensive legislation and regulation designed to prevent such malpractice. The prudent response to evasion of minimum-wage legislation, for example, is very severe punishment of the company and strengthened mechanisms to enforce the legislation. The same is true, by analogy, of many other topics on this list, most of which are recurrent problems in business ethics. We do not need the idea of CSR to remind us of these obvious truths. The remaining problems, in developed economies like the UK, are practical not conceptual. We need to get better at forcing recalcitrant companies to obey their legal duties rather than appeal to their better nature. There is a problem because these few rogue employers – and taken as a proportion of British management they are a very small number indeed – do not have a better nature.

Some of the questions on that long list, such as the extent to which employees are involved in decision making, are actually operational decisions. Advocates of CSR are actually making rather grand claims. They are suggesting that the money generated under corporate cover is, at least in part, theirs to use. The principal argument that has been put in support of this unappealing thesis is the business case.

The business case for corporate social responsibility

The business case for CSR runs as follows. Companies that obey the long list of requirements will make more money than those that do not. If this were true, if business would benefit, strictly materially, from CSR practice, then it will just happen anyway. The argument has been reduced to a simple banality: reputation matters in markets. It is now sometimes profitable to be seen to be, and sometimes actually to be, responsible actors. Therefore, to be an effective capitalist and to be a proponent of CSR is exactly the same thing.

This argument has one obvious flaw: it is not true. The very idea of a social market, of companies being embedded in social relations, which is the origin of the subject of business ethics, implies that capitalism has some drastic and undesirable outcomes. If one believes the business case for CSR, one has to give up this basic insight, which, apart from the ample historical evidence to support it, has always been the staple left-of-centre critique of capitalism. The 'business case' lets companies off far too lightly.

Business ethics

None of this leads to the conclusion that companies have no social role nor that they can meaningfully be set adrift from wider society. On the contrary, no sophisticated market economy is imaginable without a wide network of social institutions. Markets depend on non-market institutions for the skills their people have, for the regulations that prevent exploitation of monopoly positions, for the trust and the legal force that backs up contracts, to specify only three instances. As I argued earlier, the distinction between the market on the one hand and the state on the other is always false. Markets and politics are always intertwined. Hence, companies *are* part of the public realm and that imposes obligations on them. Companies also have to share public space and there are externalities, such as pollution, that arise incidentally to their business. We all bear these costs. Companies do not operate in an island called a market, so in a limited sense they do bear some responsibility for what they do.

However, these obligations need to be specified very carefully. The task at hand is still essentially to frame a set of rules that capture these costs and ascribe proportionate cost to action. The obligations of a company are, essentially, to obey all labour market regulations, to pay for *all* costs, internal and external, of their production and to work within all other legal frameworks that are relevant to them. If their practice is unsatisfactory on any of these counts, this is a case for changing the law. We should make no appeal to CSR if we believe the minimum wage is too low or that environmental pollution is taking place. These are not questions to be settled by the goodwill of the perpetrators.

Philanthropy

CSR is a simpler topic than the confused discussion makes it seem. Oddly, the second component of my definition, philanthropy, is usually excluded from discussions. Most advocates of the doctrine seem at pains to say that philanthropy is emphatically *not* what they mean by CSR. To which I would say: well, it should be. I would go further: most of the money spent on pursuing muddled CSR objectives, for which there is precious little genuine enthusiasm in companies, would be better gathered in a big collection and given to charity.

There is no need to bother with a specious business case. The very nature of philanthropy is that the interests of the company are not paramount. As soon as a business case can be established, it is business and not philanthropy. This was once a widespread corporate practice. The 19th-century non-conformists, especially the chocolate philanthropists, gave money to charitable foundations, usually out of a sense of *noblesse oblige* and religious conviction. Enlightened employers, like the Rowntrees and Leverhulmes, went way beyond the requirements of commerce in providing for their employees. They did what they did because they felt it was right. It is time we re-asserted that moral pressure. Distribute your wealth a little, not because it is in your economic interests to do so, but because it is right to do so. How strange moral arguments sound these days. They seem to have been systematically trumped by economic arguments. We have lost confidence in arguing that companies ought to act out of a sense of collective good, for no other reason than that some good would flow from the result.

These arguments will not work for that small portion of British management whose better natures are so poorly developed that they need watching to check that they are complying with the minimum wage. But, as I said, they are few in number. The bulk of people in British companies are perfectly available to hear and be persuaded by moral arguments. The 'business case' for CSR makes this more difficult because it legitimises the notion that economic imperatives are the most important.

The current corporate contribution to charitable giving in the UK is very poor indeed. Of the total income generated by charities in 2001, less than a quarter came from the corporate world. Individuals contributed almost a half. A recent report by the Social Market Foundation (SMF) (Egan, 2002) showed that individual charity is notably regressive: the poor give a greater proportion of their incomes than the rich. The focus of the government's Giving Campaign needs to be to alter this fact, at the same time as increasing the overall amount of money offered. The best way to do this is to encourage corporate philanthropy.

The overall level of corporate charitable giving in the UK is less than 1%. In the US, it is 2%. The Giving Campaign has begun the process of changing this, but it is individuals who are responding with largesse. British businesses now give an average of only 0.2% of pre-tax profit to charities and community projects, according to a survey published in *The Guardian*. The biggest 100 companies donate 0.4% of pre-tax profits, still less than half the average of their counterparts in the US. A great deal of social and community good would be done if this average were to rise from 0.4% to 1%.

Conclusion

There are not many new ideas. Most 'new' ideas are old ideas wearing fashionable clothes. I hope to have supplemented one old idea (CSR), which is suddenly very fashionable with another old idea (philanthropy) that is rather *infra dig*. If we could revive the latter then the excitement generated by the former might then be justified. For all the boring blather of government websites, it is still the right use of money that counts.

Reference

Egan, B. (2002) *Widow's might*, London: SMF.

11

Reducing inequality

Polly Toynbee

Polly Toynbee is a political and social commentator for *The Guardian*.
Her most recent book is *Hard work: Life in low pay Britain*
(Bloomsbury, 2003).

In future times looking back on the last quarter of a century, historians will see the pattern of the distribution of income and wealth and wonder at how little debate there was at the time over its extraordinary fluctuations. Why were the politics of these times so little exercised about the most fundamental economic facts upon which all its social programmes were built?

The economic history of the last century was one of almost continuous progress towards a more equal distribution of income. (Ownership of wealth is a more complicated story.) From 1900 to 1978, the annual income gap from top to bottom of society narrowed. But in the last quarter of the century, it soared away into an ever-widening gap, with no prospect of any restraint or diminishing of this dangerous trajectory.

Does it matter? On coming to power, still cautious about alarming the City and business, New Labour said loudly and often that it did not. While determined to pull up the poorest, Tony Blair always said there was no problem about how 'successful' those at the top might be. Class envy and Denis Healey's "squeezing the rich until the pips squeaked" was a dead and failed agenda of Old Labour. Although she left top rates of tax at 60% for her first eight years, Mrs Thatcher did immediately cut top tax rates by a sharp 34% which at a stroke gave a huge burst of extra income to the top earners. Top tax rates have stayed among the lowest in the Western world ever since. It is not just tax rates but also low inflation that have fuelled the widening income gap across the West.

There is an overwhelming reason why Labour will have to think again about this question. In the most radical pledge that any British politician ever made, Tony Blair promised to abolish all child poverty by the year 2020. Through introducing a minimum wage and above all through greatly increased social security for children with generous tax credits topping up incomes in low-paid families, the quarter-way mark towards that goal will almost certainly be reached by 2005, with at least 1.1 million children lifted out of poverty – a remarkable achievement. But on present policies, it will be very difficult to reach the halfway mark by 2010. As for total abolition, nothing in present strategy begins to suggest it is possible to achieve. Economists cannot see how it can be done in a society shaped as Britain's is currently.

The poverty measure used in Britain is, rightly, the same as that used right across the EU. The poor are those living below 60% of median income, the mid-way point where half the population earns less and half earns more. While the income gap widens, the government is shooting at an ever-moving target, running up a down escalator in a contest it is bound to lose. It has to see the poor keep up with the middle earners, but if the top earners are rocketing into the stratosphere, the middle earners will not stay constant for more of the poor to catch up. Either the government has to abandon its poverty abolition ambitions or the divergence of incomes has to be constrained.

The poor need not always be with us. Poverty is not an inevitable result of capitalism. Sweden and other Nordic nations have no poor, as measured by this EU scale. How have they done it? Over many decades, they have made decisions that gave a high priority to a high level of social security, a strong welfare state and universal high-quality childcare catching children at risk of failure very young. To pay for it they have high taxation. Their prices are also high, reflecting reasonable wages to lower skilled workers so there is less of a divide between the doctor and the dishwasher, less social division in where and how they live and more social cohesion.

Are these countries in some way exceptional? All kinds of explanations have been put forward about the type of society and traditions of these small Northern nations, so different from Britain. But in the end it boils down to very different political decisions taken over a long period of time with the general consent of their people. Traditionally, it has done them no economic harm. On the contrary, these nations have a GDP per capita Britain could only envy.

What's more, they are not only richer and more socially successful, they are also happier. Professor Sir Richard Layard is only one of a generation of economists in Europe and America who have begun to turn their attentions away from money onto happiness. How much happiness does money buy in what kind of societies? How can governments purchase the most happiness for their people? The results show conclusively in study after study that the West's most equal societies are also their happiest, the most unequal the most unhappy. Where the balance in individual expenditure gets out of kilter, inequality becomes dysfunctional for the whole community.

In the post-Thatcher era, the idea that there is essentially only one successful model of capitalism has taken a grim hold on Western political thought. It is a neo-conservative, US-based ideology that rejects a social democratic model. It was this unfettered free-market ideology that did so much harm to the USSR after the fall of the iron curtain. But there is no single Western model and different countries have made very different choices over the years. Plot on a graph the levels of social spending, the total tax takes, the poverty rates, social mobility, productivity and GDP and it becomes plain how many different choices different countries have made. Britain rates at the bottom for most of these measures, although it is high on employment, with France and Germany in the middle and the Nordic nations at the top. The US rates lowest of all on all scores but GDP and productivity. However, in a nation where 40% of people are too poor to have health insurance, a society so fractured by the gap between the top and bottom, the notion of an 'average' per capita income is virtually meaningless. It is like combining the economies of a third world and a first world country and averaging them together as though they all lived in the same society.

There are no iron laws of economics that decide how incomes should be distributed, but there are important political choices. This is a simple fact that goes largely undiscussed in Britain, still weighed down in the There Is No Alternative dogmas of the 1980s. It is time these genuine choices were openly debated and people realised that the shape and the happiness of society does rest in their own hands, not in some dismal globalised inevitability.

So, when it comes to trying to think imaginatively about 'the right use of money', first people need to know something more about the different paths other countries have taken, often more successfully. They need to know there are realistic choices: it is not either communism or free markets. Questions need to be put in an open-minded way. Ask this: in the last 30 years, Britain's GDP and average incomes doubled, but did we get the best value for that growth in national wealth? Could it have been better spent to increase general well-being? Was it right that the lowest two deciles stayed static or fell back while all this growth was enjoyed quite disproportionately by the highest deciles? Is that what voters actually intended and willed?

In the last 10 years, we got 30% richer as a nation. Was that well used? Or could we think of far better ways to spend the next 30% increase in the next 10 years? More four-wheel drive sports utility vehicles or more beautiful parks, public spaces and public buildings? By holding back the growth among the above-average earners – not by cuts in anyone's income – we could have beautiful schools and magnificent local sports and leisure centres to be proud of. We could have museums, galleries, arts, drama and music centres open all hours. We could have Sure Start Children's Centres for every child, as well-equipped and well-staffed as palaces in every neighbourhood where mothers would go from ante-natal check-ups through to primary school with affordable childcare and nursery teaching so every child gets an early step up and all women could work who wanted to. Now add in here any of the public glories that would immeasurably improve the life of communities, from good public transport to safe urban streets.

The question is how to raise the public ambitions of voters who have been given mean and narrow visions of what is possible. The individualistic 'You will always spend your own money far better than the state ever will' is a counsel of despair, implying all government is bad, all taxes always wasted. However, ask people what matters to them most for their own family and for the country and they will always cite those things that are best bought collectively – good schools, good doctors, safe communities, a good environment, things for their children and teenagers to do and a spirit of neighbourliness.

A culture that encourages everyone to hold on to what they've got and the devil-take-the-hindmost can never deliver these things that people say they want most. Only higher taxes can deliver these things – and people know it. Yet they look across the channel and see clean, proud towns and transport that works after years of higher taxes, but often fail to connect the cause and effect. People know they only get what they pay for in life – but they are easily discouraged, fearing they will pay the tax and still not get what they pay for. Breaking this cycle of distrust in government is essential.

The commissioning of the Wanless report on the state of the NHS was an excellent example of a way to open discussion of the public sector deficit, prove the need, prescribe the remedy and gain sufficient trust to raise and spend extra money well. Raising National Insurance by 1p for the NHS was remarkably acceptable to voters, once the explanation was there for all to scrutinise. To ask what is 'the right use of money' is to open up this tax debate in more creative, less negative terms right across the board.

Apart from gaining consent to a higher tax regime, there needs to be a debate on pay and relative rewards. Now that the biggest single group of the poor are in work, the injustice of rewards is more apparent than ever. Why does a care assistant looking after the frail earn too little to survive on? Why is the director's pay out of control at the top, when he no more inhabits an international market for his talents than the care assistant?

The government has striven to improve the lot of the low paid. Despite dire warnings from the Confederation of British Industry (CBI) and others, the minimum wage was introduced and benefited over a million, mainly women, workers with no job losses. But it remains at a very modest £4.50 an hour. It is far below even the most conservative estimate of a living wage – probably around £6.30, according to various academic estimates. Could it be raised safely? Almost certainly, until such a point where there was evidence that jobs were being lost. Then there could be a return to the Wages

Councils abolished in the 1980s. These set minimum wages for each sector: safe levels will differ widely between manufacturing and catering, for example. A higher minimum wage would mean prices would rise, but the case needs to be put that if the dishwasher in the restaurant where you eat cannot live on the wages she gets, then the price of the meal is too low, since the government and the taxpayer picks up the rest of the bill by subsidising those low wages with tax credits.

The government itself controls a powerful part of the labour market. If it wanted to raise pay in the bottom two deciles of earners, it could fix a separate public sector minimum wage (also applicable to contracted-out workers), which would be a strong influence on all jobs in the private sector without imposing a mandatory high rate on every local hairdresser. To do this, more taxpayers' money would have to go into public sector pay. A general understanding would need to be canvassed for improving public sector pay, which still remains on average far behind the private sector. But this needs governmental advocacy, since otherwise the opposition points to rising public wages as money 'wasted'. All these strategies require public explanation and support for greater equity.

There are other ways governments can influence pay structures. Establishing a norm for the relative distance between the top and bottom wage within any organisation would help, with an obligation to explain to shareholders why, if the norm has been broken. A rule of thumb 30 years ago was that the top to bottom in most companies was a factor of around ten times, according to Income Data Services. Now it can be 200 times and more. Naming and shaming with public proclamations about what is right and fair can do far more than timid politicians realise to change climates of opinion and habits on pay.

Absolute transparency in pay would be a crucial first step in shifting attitudes towards a more just pay structure. Every employee in every organisation should always know exactly where they stand in the pecking order – and why. The paranoia that others are getting more often fuels rising pay at the top. Ignorance often allows groups of workers, women especially, to be paid less without realising. Breaking coyness and taboos over pay packets would be a shock at first, but people would soon learn how secrecy over money tends to hide both shamefully high and shamefully low pay rates, alongside great irregularities and unevenness.

The government prefers to redistribute money through tax credits to the poorest families than to engage with the trickier wages question. Tax credits have been generous and have been largely responsible for lifting the first quarter of poor families out of poverty. But already there is a suspicion they are depressing wage rates at the bottom, without employers realising their low pay is being heavily subsidised. To vastly increase tax credit rates to reach the next tranche of poor families would grossly distort the market. It would also deliver ever-stranger pay packets, where the majority of pay came from benefits and only a small part from hard work in vital jobs, cleaning hospitals and streets or caring for old people. So if the government intends to reach its ambitious poverty targets, it cannot do it by stealthy tax credits alone. A more equal distribution of pay rates has to be tackled sooner rather than later.

None of this is an economic impossibility. What holds back the present government is fear that it is political suicide. As a result of this anxiety, the argument is never put, the vision never described. Hiding behind the cloak of globalised inevitabilities, talk of high taxes and fairer pay is regarded as just too dangerous.

It may well be that civil society, the voluntary sector, think tanks and organisations like the Friends Provident Charitable Foundation are in a better position to start a mature debate along theses lines, engaging opinion formers, the City, trade unions, the CBI, but above all the public in discussions about what is fair; point-scoring in House of Commons party politics dare not discuss it. Fair reward and the nature of merit is the fundamental political question of our times. It is a shocking fact that social mobility has all but ground to a halt and birth is again destiny as it was at the start of the last century.

Any debate on 'the right use of money' must include building some coherent pattern out of a pay structure now grown grossly dysfunctional to create a social structure of opportunity and just reward for work.

Part Four: Empowerment

The chapters in this section concentrate on using money in ways that empower individuals directly. They emphasise the need to listen carefully to, and value, the views of the recipients of money, responding to the particular requirements of diverse community cultures. The first chapter here expresses the view of someone living on a low income. The chapters that then follow suggest approaches that may help empower people within modern-day financial, economic and social systems.

Moraene Roberts describes, from the viewpoint of someone living on a low income, the disempowering impact of having little money in a world where people are likely to be valued – and respected – on the basis of what they own. She suggests that it is critical to respect the human rights of each and every person and that a society that really does start from this point would be more likely to use money in ways that optimise the potential of every individual. Her overall conclusion is that money invested in people in order to allow them to be full participants in society is money well and justly spent.

Dorothy Rowe shows how each of us has our own way of seeing things and how difficult it can be for us to put aside our own ideas and really understand those of others. Yet, unless we undertake such hard work, giving can do more harm than good.

Understanding and responding to the real needs of a culturally diverse population is the central theme of **Ram Gidoomal**. The right use of money will vary depending on cultural and religious values. For example, an imperative to provide a dowry will affect savings decisions, what to invest in and so on. He provides examples of projects at the local level that encourage a good use of money in ways that respond to particular community needs.

Matthew Pike writes that the right use of money needs to take account of the realities that poor people face in disadvantaged areas. He emphasises that helplessness is not conquered simply by providing more money, but by encouraging investment in the full range of a community's assets: physical, human, social, cultural, knowledge and so on, as well as the more traditional financial assets. In particular, he suggests that a good use of money is to invest in projects that lever in more of these assets or make those already there more productive.

Niall Cooper concentrates particularly on the financial services and instruments that could empower people in poor communities. He offers a range of options for ensuring that the full range of financial services is available to poorer people.

12

Living on a low income

Moraene Roberts

Moraene Roberts has had long-term direct experience of living in
poverty. As an activist with the human rights-based organisation, ATD
Fourth World, she now writes and speaks regularly on poverty and
rights issues. Currently she is promoting the participation of people
living in poverty in policy planning and research. She is also involved
in a project developing a module for use in the training of social
workers.

I found it a strange question to ask someone who has lived on a
very low income for years, 'What does the phrase *the right use of
money* mean to you?'. My first thought was that I would need to
have more than just barely enough money to meet the basics of life
before I could begin to think of right and wrong uses of money.

I use money to survive, to exist and to fight for the right to have
more in order to be able to do more. As a member of the human
rights-based, anti-poverty organisation ATD Fourth World, my
children and I have been given support for 14 years. This has enabled
me to face the struggle against poverty and social exclusion knowing
that I have others alongside me. It has given me strength to fight
for my family and the opportunities to see that fight in the context
of personal responsibility and social policy. I have the opportunity
of meeting often with others who also struggle in their daily lives,
to analyse our situations and find how this relates to government
policies and local initiatives.

There is a lot of public debate at present about the reality of
poverty as experienced by families in Britain, or if in fact poverty
exists in Britain at all. One of the most frequently heard phrases is,
"It is not just about lack of money", and, of course, this is absolutely

true. The families who are involved with ATD Fourth World say all the time that it is about how one feels treated; about respect and recognition of one's effort and struggles. It is also true that if you can afford to look, dress, act and speak like someone who can afford to be confident in life, you get treated with respect automatically. So perhaps the role of income inadequacy in keeping people in lifelong poverty must not be underestimated.

In the world we currently live in, we are far more likely to be valued by what we own than by who we really are and what we do. This then gives us a sense of our self-worth that is based on the values and behaviour of others. Children who hear their parents constantly referred to as 'dole scroungers' or 'shirkers' will find it hard to feel proud of their origins or to grow up with real aspirations. One little boy, eagerly awaiting the birth of his brother, told me how he was scared to say that his mother was having another baby because the neighbours were always making comments about her. What messages are we giving the children of poor parents about how welcome they are in our world?

Poverty exists in every country. In some it is poverty to the point of death; in others it pushes some people to the margins and leaves them there. Poverty exists in Britain now. What are the realities of living in poverty today? Not having enough money means not having any choices in most aspects of life. You cannot choose where you live, where your children go to school, where you shop, nor can you afford to be an eco-friendly or a fair trade consumer. What others may consider normal – such as an occasional holiday or outing for the whole family together, buying clothes new or having more than one pair of shoes – is just not possible for the millions of people who experience life in poverty. At worse, living in poverty can mean not being seen as able to look after your children and having them taken from you and put in care.

According to the people I meet with at ATD Fourth World's monthly policy forums, one of the hardest things to bear is being blamed for your situation by people who do not understand the difficulties and complexities of your life. This is especially true for those who do not dip in and out of poverty as they dip in and out of work, but rather exist between various levels of poverty regardless of whether they are working or not. People in this situation are always in receipt of full or top-up benefits and so are never free from the scrutiny and comments of others.

There is a real double standard around the use of money depending on whose money it is. If money is earned, you are free to spend it how you wish – even to the detriment of your health or of the ecology. Not so if it is a payment from the state; then, any taxpayer can feel free to judge you on how you spend "my hard-earned cash". One clear demonstration of this was when a friend of mine rang to tell me that she had just become a grandmother. She was thrilled and gushed about how wonderful it would be to "have Alison and Ashleigh home with us". Her daughter's boyfriend had left and my friend and her husband were going to support her until Alison was up to going back to work, which could be a year or two. I mentioned that another young woman I knew had also just had a baby, to which she retorted that, "Knowing her, it will be just another child from a one-parent family that the state will be expected to keep". Not for one second did she consider that, there but for having well-to-do parents, stood her own daughter.

I am often amazed at how someone will buy a drink for a friend who has serious health problems, but refuse to give money to a homeless person because, "They will only buy alcohol and get ill". I know people who will give cigarettes to their friends and loved ones but not to the homeless because it is "bad for them anyway". I have also often experienced being told that I have an excuse for getting benefits because I am disabled, but that those who beg in the streets have no such excuse and should get a job. This usually from people who know little of my life and abilities and none at all of the lives of those who sit under the cash dispensers at the supermarket. No one should feel that they have the right to make uninformed judgements on other human beings since to do so dehumanises both parties.

We are a rich nation that is led by politicians (of all major parties) who are terrified to suggest redistribution of wealth in order to fight social inequality and poverty. I am ashamed of how we have moved from the language of Social Security to that of Welfare. Instead of being proud of our system that offers help to the most vulnerable, we blame, accuse and resent them. The misuse of the system by a few has created a deep mistrust of the many – and this divides us as a nation. We should be looking to build a society that uses money to optimise the potential of every individual through respecting human rights. Instead we are spending money on investigating, policing and oppressing those who have the hardest lives.

All of this makes those of us who want to contribute time and energy to voluntary work reluctant to try. Our access to benefits, especially housing benefit, is fragile and easily cancelled at the suspicion of any illegal working. In my own case, I write and speak about poverty and social exclusion but am not able to earn nearly enough to get off benefits and so cannot use the skills I have to earn any money. Like many others, I make a contribution to our society by offering emotional and practical support to those who need it and by trying to find ways to be a good friend and neighbour. These are efforts that are essential for a cohesive society and yet they have no financial value and so are ignored.

There is a myth that work equals wealth and independence. Some people work all their lives at low-paid, low-status jobs that have an adverse effect on their health and self-respect, without ever being out of debt or free from worry about money. How can some companies pay more per year for one managing director than for all of the cleaning, catering and part-time workers put together? As a society, we seem capable of defining work only as paid employment; this devalues work done without pay. When I see people standing out in all weathers selling the *Big Issue*, I often think that I would hate to do that job, because I see it as a job. Every day millions of people do practical things that benefit others, without it being recognised as work. A grandmother I know looked after her elderly, sick husband and her three grandchildren. This allowed her daughters to work and also relieved the pressure on local health services, yet she was seen as unemployed and therefore not working. Many charities rely heavily on the contribution of volunteers and volunteering can be a pathway back to employment, especially after illness, but volunteers are often dismissed as not working. At the same time, some volunteers have even been harassed for doing unpaid 'work' while on benefits.

When people in very hard circumstances try to improve their positions, they are often misunderstood and accused. A man I knew well had been unemployed for a long time in spite of attending many courses to build his skills and get some qualifications. He was often refused jobs due to lack of work experience and so offered to do some painting and decorating for a couple of elderly people, without pay, in return for a reference from them. A 'concerned citizen', responding to government advertising, reported him to the Benefits Agency without even bothering to speak to him first. As a result, he faced weeks of intrusive and distressing questions and investigation. Fearful that he would be plunged into housing arrears and lose his little flat, he was almost at the point of suicide by the time that the matter was resolved.

So often those who know them little, and care about them less, inflict the deepest scars born by poor and excluded people. Worse still, are when those scars are inflicted by the very people employed to help and support, who use their positions of power inappropriately. It is so very easy to pass judgement on the basis of very little information and on where people are at when we first meet them. It takes time and trust to develop knowledge of a person's struggles and efforts and the problems that bring them to the attention of statutory agencies.

In the case of many families I meet, the prime agency is social services. This should be the first point of call for families in difficulty, but in truth there is a real fear of asking for help. This fear may be unrealistic, but is sometimes based in personal experience. Among the people who come to ATD Fourth World, many of us have been in local authority care as children, had children taken into care or have faced years of battling to keep our children with us. The main reason given for removal of children from backgrounds of poverty is neglect. Lack of life skills; *failure to show emotion*; lack of financial means; inadequate housing; *inability to provide stability*; social isolation; and *not getting children to school* being just some of the criteria by which a parent's ability to parent may be measured. Most of these can be alleviated by offering services designed to keep the family together but all too often this option is not available. One social worker told me, "Of course it is poverty but we call it neglect because we can't do anything about a child's poverty except move them out of it". Another told me that the main problems for children in care are being moved around (*inability to provide stability*), not getting an education (*not getting children to school*) and being looked after by people who do not care about you (*failure to show emotion*). These are some of the same reasons given for taking the children away from their parents in the first place. With all the resources at their disposal, social services cannot do much better.

Removing the children of poor families into care therefore does not guarantee that they are safe from poverty in the long term. In spite of the huge cost of the services for children in care, there is an abundance of reports that show the poor outcomes in terms of life chances for those children. These indicate the disproportionately high number of care-leavers in figures on homelessness, mental illness, imprisonment, drug and alcohol abuse, prostitution and suicide. These are some of the measurable effects; it is impossible to estimate the emotional cost paid by children in care, their parents and their siblings. One young person said, "Everyone thinks I was in care because I was a bad kid or had a bad mother. Neither was true but it is a stigma I will have to carry all my life". Family support services have been cut to the bone and services for children and families are completely child-protection led, especially in the wake of the tragic deaths of a number of children in recent years. One social work student told me recently, "I chose this profession to try to help families but it is almost impossible. No help is offered until the family reaches crisis point and then we jump all over them with questions and rules. I am debating if I have chosen right".

When a child is taken away because of neglect, many people assume that it is because of physical or sexual abuse by the parents. This leaves parents not just with the devastating loss of their child but also at the mercy of gossipmongers and public opinion when they are at their lowest point. There is often no one close enough to these people to support them or speak up for them and so they suffer alone. The ongoing support of a social worker or voluntary sector worker can make all the difference but usually services end once the child is no longer in the family. I never cease to be amazed at the capacity of one human being to kick another when they are down. When you spend your whole life down, you take a lot of kicks. What is it in some of us that allows us to hurt others and to ignore great injustice, as long as we are not the ones who suffer it?

The experience of many families is that the training, good practice and attitude of individual social workers can make the difference as to whether a child stays at home or is removed. A large number of excellent and very experienced social workers have either left the profession due to stress or disillusionment, or moved into government initiatives such as Sure Start. This has had a dramatic impact on the level and quality of services available to the most vulnerable parents and their children. ATD Fourth World and the Family Rights Group are working with Royal Holloway University of London, Luton University, the Social Care Institute For Excellence, the Department of Health, social work practitioners and people living in poverty who are in touch with social services to design a module for use in the training of social workers. The core element of this module is that people who experience poverty and have been users of children and family services will be training student and post-qualifying social workers on the reality of poverty and the traditional connection between poverty and the removal of children into care. This will hopefully lead to an increase in good practice, supportive services and a reduction of children being taken away from their families.

Such a project should attract funding from all quarters, yet it does not. For ATD Fourth World, which does not play the victim card with people's dignity, funding is a huge problem. They believe in listening and learning from those at the sharp end of society's problems and trying to empower and encourage them to find their voice and access their rights in order to make a contribution to society. If they provided standard services to teach employment skills or get people back into work, they would be able to access many sources of funding; but mainstream services find it difficult to reach the most marginalised groups. Yet organisations whose approach is about bringing together people who come from different backgrounds, who might never otherwise meet, to build a common fight against poverty and a fairer and more equal society, find funders are few and far between. Those who have funded ATD Fourth World have provided the means for so many to learn about their rights and their social responsibilities, to find friendship and support and to become better engaged with society. In some cases, the support given has helped to keep children with their parents, for others, to cope with the loss and survive. This is a good use of money. Money that is invested in people in order to allow them to be full participants in society is money well and justly spent.

At the start of writing this I wondered what I, and others like me, could contribute to a debate on the right use of money. Now I know that, if those with the least access to money and the most difficulties were asked this question as part of an ongoing dialogue, we could begin to build together with others the means to eradicate poverty and to have a society to be truly proud of.

13

Hearing but not listening: why charities fail

Dorothy Rowe

Dorothy Rowe is a psychologist and writer. Her books include *The real meaning of money.* All her work is based on the research into the operation of the brain and the senses of perception which shows that, since we are physically incapable of seeing reality directly, we are always engaged in creating interpretations or meanings. Since such meanings can come only from our experience, and since no two people ever have the same experience, no two people ever see anything in exactly same way. It is on this basis that Dorothy Rowe analyses why we behave as we do.

Vast sums of donors' money have been wasted because the donors did not take the time and trouble to understand how the people they wanted to help saw themselves and their world. Gaining such an understanding usually threatens the donors' world view, and so they prefer to believe that they know best. We often see the same thing happen in our personal lives.

I was ill recently, nothing life-threatening but it was quite debilitating with intermittent bouts of severe pain. Two friends, separately, chose to help me. Without asking me, the first friend decided what it was that I needed. I found myself side-lined and, from the way she was treating me, I feared that my friend thought that I had become senile. Meanwhile she created havoc around me. Finally she departed, and I was left to pick up the pieces. The following week, still ill, I went to visit the other friend. She listened carefully to my account of my illness and she observed me closely. She learned very quickly to see the change in my expression that indicated that the pain was returning. Then, without fuss, comment or advice, she made everything simple and comfortable for me. We lived quietly, talking when I wanted to talk, being quiet when I wanted to be quiet. When I expressed an interest in having some soup she unobtrusively prepared a bowl of soup that was nourishing and comforting. She laughingly assured me that making soup was a selfish act because there was nothing she enjoyed more than cooking for other people. I left her home feeling comforted and physically much better.

The difference between my first and second friend lay in the way each of them had interpreted the situation. My first friend believed that she knew more about me than I knew about myself and that in helping me, she was showing herself to be both competent and virtuous. My second friend believed that she had to learn from me what it was that I needed.

My experience of these two kinds of help were, in microcosm, the experience of millions of people who, having been seen by charitable institutions as being needy, were on the receiving end of 'help'. The fortunate ones were those who encountered charities who operated like my second friend. Their way of working was first to get to understand the people they proposed to support. They lived with them, learning their language and coming to understand how they saw themselves and their world. They observed these people's way of life closely and saw how what they could offer would fit into the pattern of their lives. They made no decisions until they had discussed the matter thoroughly with the people themselves. Help was a joint enterprise, not the act of one group of people doing good to another group.

The unfortunate objects of charitable 'help' were those people who encountered charity organisers who believed that they knew what was best for other people. Such organisers wasted no time learning about the people they were proposing to spend money on, people whom they saw as ignorant, primitive savages or the passive victims of some oppressive religion or political regime or of natural disaster. So puffed up were the organisers with their pride in themselves, they failed to realise that what they were doing was, at best, useless and, at worst, destructive.

I have been observing the functions of charities, either government organisations or private charities, since the end of the Second World

War when European governments withdrew, one by one, from the African states that they had dominated for a hundred years or more. There were grand ceremonies and self-congratulatory statements about the vast sums of money government and businesses were giving to the new African leaders, supposedly to create democratic structures that would benefit their people. Such gifts were based on a failure of observation, the tragic consequences of which are still with us today.

The new African states were based on the artificial divisions of the continent created by European governments in their greedy, ruthless scramble for a share of the land and its wealth. European leaders took no account of what Africans themselves saw as the appropriate borders between different groups, and they ignored or used for their own benefit long-standing enmities between different tribes. Moreover, they failed to observe that the basic economy of Africa rested on African women. Relatively few African men were involved in trade although considerably more were employed as cheap labour for European-owned industries, but it was the women who tilled the soil and sold the produce while caring for their families. Most African men meanwhile were engaged in the important activities of gossiping, singing and dancing, sex, sport, jockeying for power, and fighting among themselves. Finding themselves in possession of vast sums of money the leaders of such men squandered it on corruption and lavish spending on themselves and on the weapons of war. The arms trade conducted by the Western governments, particularly by Britain, the US and Russia, was soon flourishing, as were the increasingly bitter conflicts in Africa. Meanwhile, the women worked harder and grew poorer as their economy was disrupted and destroyed, and they lost their land.

The tragedy of Africa is perhaps the most spectacular example of the failures of charitable enterprises, but it was not the only tragedy. In other parts of the world, people have suffered enormously from the 'gift' of a hydroelectric scheme which resulted in millions of people losing their land, or a 'gift' of a state-of-the-art hospital which was too high-tech to treat the diseases indigenous to that locality.

However, it is not surprising that most people, and not merely those who would claim to do good, are reluctant to undertake the onerous and often destabilising course of trying to understand how other people see themselves and the world. We like to tell ourselves that all sensible people see the world as we do, and that anyone who does not share our views is either mad or bad, but once we start to investigate other people's views we soon discover that no one else sees the world exactly as we do. This is inevitable, because the way we are constructed physiologically means that such differences in viewpoint are inevitable.

The ancient Greek philosopher Epictatus once remarked, "It is not things in themselves that trouble us, but our opinions of things". Neuroscientists who study how the brain works have now shown that we are incapable of seeing 'things in themselves'. All we can know are our 'opinions of things'. We each create our own individual picture of ourselves as well as the world we live in. This picture comes out of our past experience and, since no two people ever have the same experience, no two people ever see any event in exactly the same way. Epictatus can now be re-stated as, "What determines our behaviour isn't what happens to us but how we interpret what happens to us". Thus, in trying to be charitable we might think we are helping another person but, if the person being helped does not perceive what we do as help, then it is not help.

Before we set out to offer aid to anyone we need to determine how that person sees their own situation. We should also ask ourselves *why* we want to offer this help. Companies who engage in sponsorship are very clear about whom and what they sponsor. The sponsorship is aimed at appealing to a well-defined group of customers and at enhancing the reputation of the company and its products. In our charitable enterprises, whether we work individually or as a group, we need to be aware of why we do what we do. As part of this we need to consider what money means to us.

Charitable enterprises usually involve money. Money is not an inert substance, in its various forms, we pass around for the convenience of trade. Money is a set of ideas, or rather two sets of ideas, one set which we share with other people and one which is our own private set of ideas. We use our shared ideas to agree, say, that this piece of paper is worth ten pounds and those figures on a computer screen mean that X number of euros can be exchanged for Y number of dollars. Important though these shared ideas may be, the individual, private ideas we have about money are even more important to us; indeed, they form a significant part of our sense of identity (Freeman, 2000).

We try to use our money to enhance how we see ourselves and to influence favourably how other people see us. Even if we believe that it is virtuous not to be interested in money, the fact that we try not to think about money makes our idea of money an important part of our identity. If we like to think of ourselves as being generous, we can assure ourselves that we are generous by giving money to charity. If we want other people to *see* us as being generous, we try to make sure that people know about it. Our private ideas about money can change over our lifetime. One person, born to feckless parents, may resolve to devote his life to making money in order to feel safe. However, when he reaches a point in his life where he realises that he cannot live long enough to spend his wealth, he may alter his priorities and decide that he now wants history to record his existence not as a very successful entrepreneur but as a great public benefactor.

No individual or company is so wealthy as to be able to support every good cause, and in fact no one ever tries to. We select which charities we shall support according to our assessment of ourselves and of our world. Such assessments are often based on very little knowledge. It is much easier to raise money for charities for blind people than for deaf people because people who are neither blind nor deaf often sentimentalise blind people but find deaf people strange and difficult. Similarly, more money goes to charities that promote physical health rather than mental health. We can all imagine how horrible it would be to have cancer or heart disease, but, as I have learned from my work with depressed people, there are many non-depressed people who believe that depression is catching just as the SARS virus is catching. They feel that just giving money to a mental health charity could put them in peril.

Many people support and even may set up a charity which relates to some traumatic experience of their own. Such a charity may meet a currently unmet need in the community, but there is always the danger that the people involved in the charity are so close to the particular need that they cannot assess impartially alternative interpretations of the problem and its cure.

Most of the fierce controversies that rage within a charity are about value judgements to do with money and with our need to be virtuous. No one ever dares to say out loud that what he or she is fighting over is the high moral ground to which they lay claim. Rather, many people who strive to be good lie to themselves about what they are actually doing. They tell themselves that they are behaving altruistically, that they have no personal motive for doing good. As children they have been taught that this is what they ought to do. They have never realised that total altruism is an ideal that no one can ever reach. We can choose to be unselfish as against choosing to be selfish, but in making that choice we meet our prime need of being able to think well of ourselves and have other people think well of us. We have to try to meet this need because life is intolerable if we cannot think reasonably well of ourselves and have satisfactory relationships with at least a few people who hold us in high regard.

Understanding that altruism is impossible allows us to move from blind selfishness to what Bertrand Russell called 'enlightened self-interest', which is the ability to order our priorities according to what in the long term will matter most to us. We might come to see improving the quality of other people's lives as actually improving the quality of our own. The world becomes a better place for us to live. Thus it is in our own interest to make the effort to understand how those we would help see themselves, the world they live in and the help we can offer. Only then can we be sure that what we offer actually is help.

References

Freeman, W.J. (2000) *How brains make up their minds*, London: Orion Books Ltd.

Rowe, D. (1998) *The real meaning of money*, London: HarperCollins.

14

Responding to cultural diversity

Ram Gidoomal

Ram Gidoomal is an author, entrepreneur and former UK group chief
executive of the Inlaks Group, a multinational business with 7,000
employees. He and his family were forced to leave wealth and
prosperous business interests behind them when they came to Britain
from East Africa as refugees. He began his business career in the
family corner shop in Shepherds Bush and followed this by spending a
short time as an analyst with Lloyds Bank International in the City of
London. He was Founder Trustee and Chairman of the Christmas
Cracker Charity which has given thousands of young people direct
entrepreneurial experience and which has raised over £5 million for
projects in developing countries. He serves on several boards in the
private, public and voluntary sectors.

[Earth's problem was]: most of the people living [there] were unhappy
for pretty much of the time. Many solutions were suggested for this
problem, but most of these were largely concerned with the
movements of small green pieces of paper, which is odd because on the
whole it wasn't the small green pieces of paper which were
unhappy.... (Douglas Adams, *So long, and thanks for all the fish*,
1984, p 7)

This essay will make special reference to my own South Asian
background in the context of Britain's minority ethnic
communities, which include the African, Caribbean and other
communities.

Although there are many definitions of 'money', they are essentially
different aspects of the same thing. For the economist, money is an

economic foundation. For the sociologist, it is a social good; lack of it is a social disadvantage. For the activist, it is a means of empowerment. For the social demographer, it is a medium of social mobility: inner-city gentrification is 'money moving in'.

The question of the right use of money, however, has many different answers. I came late to Western capitalism: born a Hindu, brought up a Sikh and educated in a Muslim school, I arrived in Britain as a refugee in the 1960s and encountered (and later adopted) the Christian religion. From a very early age, I realised that attitudes to money tend to be driven by cultural, religious and philosophical views.

Hindus, for example, believe that the material world is *maya* (illusion). Yet there is also a strong philanthropic tradition: care for the needy is a meritorious act, bringing karmic benefits to those who perform it. Many charities exist in the UK, founded both by well-known Hindus and by those not widely known.

Islam forbids the levying of interest, whereas in the Judeo-Christian West businesses normally function by borrowing money with interest. The Christian Parable of the Talents suggests that a proper use of assets is not to bury them in the ground, but to use them for growth. Ever since, usury has been a thorny topic in Judeo-Christianity: a needy borrower is not to be charged interest, and if he puts up his cloak as collateral, it is to be returned to him at night (Exodus 22). Nevertheless, in an inflationary society, burying money is the same as throwing some of it away.

Yet, although religious and philosophical perspectives can define local economic norms, the global village is an economic melting pot. Hinduism and other Eastern philosophies influence over two billion people, many of them in key world financial centres. Similarly, Islamic banks operating in the West have had to devise alternative ways of making up the losses incurred through inflation. The Judeo-Christian belief that all money is God-given creates a dynamic of right use that operates alongside competing ideologies.

And Asian influences are by no means the only ones. 'Western capitalism' is no longer a monolithic, wholly Western matter.

There are many ways of using money badly, as any tabloid illustrates. Even the basic economic structures have often been questioned: Keynes, for example, looked forward to a time when society would progress from necessary "avarice and usury and precaution" to "some of the most sure and certain principles of religion and traditional virtue ... that avarice is a vice ... and the love of money is detestable" (Keynes, 1932, pp 358-74).

So what is a right use of money?

Again, prescriptions for right use depend on values that go beyond economic values. Cultural, local government, national and sometimes faith issues are all involved. Some examples of cultural and faith issues are given in the next section, followed by examples relating to local government and the use of public money, before wider issues and a comment on the future conclude this piece.

Cultural and faith issues

The dowry system

The South Asian 'dowry' gives a daughter, upon marriage, her share of the family inheritance. A dowry can be the biggest factor driving the family savings philosophy. Although it is the bride's money, that is, her contribution to the marriage, some abusive husbands take it for themselves. Knowing that this can happen, parents often purchase gold and silver jewellery, expensive clothes and other non-liquid assets for their daughter, so that if the marriage fails she will have resources to fall back on. Western (and Asian) observers have sometimes questioned if this is a right use of money, in a world with so many other pressing needs.

Other issues are involved. Many families believe that providing a good dowry is a God-given duty (*dharma*) and that an inappropriate dowry will irreparably damage family honour (*izzat*). Some difficult marriages are known to have led to honour killings, kitchen-fire deaths and other tragedies. A single cultural issue affects everyday family decisions: how to save, in what to invest money, how to provide for one's children: worldview, religious belief and social convention all determine what the 'right' use of money is.

Imaginative refocusing by financial providers could play a major part in addressing this problem. For example, most banks are now well aware of the value of ethnic desks and minority language services where appropriate. The next stage might be carefully tailored programmes for issues such as dowry funding. Plans for school fees, retirement home financing and endowment policies for one's children are now commonplace. Dowry plans could not only encourage right use of family money; they could destroy the stranglehold that extortionate moneylenders sometimes have on families with dowry worries.

Mother Teresa of Calcutta provided dowries for abandoned girls in her care. In the UK (and abroad), at least one organisation exists that has a low-profile, confidential plan providing a basic dowry fund for families, enabling daughters to marry with dignity and avoiding the attentions of loan sharks. The UK's modern multicultural society needs such facilities, easily accessible and with minimal embarrassment attached to using them.

Different cultural approaches to lending and borrowing

For most ethnic communities, issues of lending and borrowing are intimately related to the question of the right use of money. Many debates in those communities implicitly challenge the conventions of Western capitalism. For example, Asian finance often relies heavily on the *hoondee* system; that is, community lending underwritten by trust, honour and a statement of intent to repay. It is guaranteed by *izzat*: if a businessman defaults on a loan, other community members will meet his debts so that the community will not be disgraced.

To address the social injustices inherent in some existing economic structures does not demand overthrowing those structures: a radical review and some lateral thinking can achieve social and economic transformation.

An example is the Boost employment bond for the City and East London, the Steering Committee of which I chaired. A zero-interest bond, it aimed to raise money for business, urban regeneration and community welfare projects in the three poorest UK boroughs (all neighbouring the City). Boost (which is one of several similar schemes) mobilised much voluntary giving of time and expertise by some of the biggest names in the City. However, its *modus operandi* required re-thinking, then working within existing structures and existing use of money. It used a conventional zero-interest voucher model, but offered a social instead of a financial dividend.

Participating City businesses were not required to become something different in order to be part of Boost, but by such means as mentoring schemes and business advisory services, the expertise of the City was made available to fledgling entrepreneurs and business start-ups in the disadvantaged neighbouring boroughs.

Micro lending is another example of a radical concept in lending to the extremely poor. The principle is that often only small loans are needed to enable the very poor to break out of the cycle of poverty: so loan poor people money on terms that are suitable to them, teach them a few sound financial principles, and they will help themselves. Mohammed Yunus' Grameen Bank, following micro-lending principles, has lent more than $2 billion to the very poor in Bangladesh. UK micro-lender, Street (UK), has considered harnessing the honour system of some minority ethnic communities to group syndicate borrowing. Ken Livingstone has raised the possibility of micro lending as an option for minority ethnic business support in London (GLA, 2003, p 44).

Initiatives like these implicitly challenge existing ways of doing economics. They have clear overtones of social justice, fairer outcomes and empowerment for borrowers. The resulting increases in the flow of money within minority and disadvantaged communities facilitate community growth. It is a viable alternative to costly venture capital funding and substantial other benefits also accrue.

Family issues in some minority ethnic communities

In many ethnic communities, the extended family is the basis of social and economic life, and the business leadership model is quite different from conventional Western models. Leadership resides in the family hierarchy; family members living abroad can have a significant say in company policy; the family as a whole owns the business's money.

As ethnic communities increasingly interact, issues like going public, recruiting executive staff from outside the family or community, and other 'right use' issues become difficult.

An entrepreneur has prospered. At the end of his life, to whom does he bequeath his business? Traditional Asian values suggest that the right use of it is to share it equally between the sons. But what if one son is an inept businessman? A number of financial houses now have plans whereby the business-incompetent son might, for example, receive a cash payment instead of a seat on the board. This is arguably a more 'right' use of money, preserving as it does not only the business-competent son's inheritance but also the jobs of the workforce and the prosperity of others with an interest in the company's success.

Legacies are a common problem, with the bequeather possibly having to juggle the 'family values of providing for relatives' and the 'desire to enjoy the applause for his philanthropy' while still alive. However this tension is resolved, there are consequences for the family business, the extended family, and the economy of the local community.

Such issues are largely unfamiliar to mainstream community business. But for the ethnic community businesses, they are both ethical and business problems. Quite apart from ethics, the business case for addressing them is very strong.

Ethnic business in the UK represents over 7% of the total small business stock and accounts for more than 9% of all start-ups. One estimate indicates that ethnic business contributes approximately 10% of the UK's total GDP. It is the entrepreneurial drive of [such] businessmen and women that help sustain and promote this nation's wealth. (Digby Jones, Director-General CBI, commenting in October 2003 on the launch of the CBI's Asian Section)

Issues of the right use of money faced by ethnic businesses affect the whole business community. Financial organisations of all kinds need to enter into this aspect of the use of money debate.

Local government and community issues

In local government, almost every act of spending money has moral and ethical implications: the right use of public money is increasingly on the agenda of local and community bodies. I work with a number of public and voluntary sector organisations, for example the London Sustainability Exchange. Topics such as the Triple Bottom Line (taking account of the economic, social and environmental consequences of a business's activities) and Socially Responsible Investment (making investment decisions on the basis of both the financial and social performance of a business) are part of our everyday vocabulary. How should wealthy businesses be encouraged, or even allowed, to use their money? How can business satisfy the interests of stakeholders as well as shareholders? Should businesses with a money surplus be allowed to spend it in ways that make life more difficult for the poor, or compromise the sustainability of the environment? Such matters recur in the annual reports and discussion documents of organisations from local industry to multinationals as well as in other local and community bodies.

For myself, I believe that businesses should be compelled to account for what they destroy as well as what they create. The community in which a business operates is a stakeholder in that company's activities. It suffers from pollution created, it benefits from environmental improvements initiated. It can benefit from health, recreation and other facilities created by businesses for their employees – or it can be excluded and still pay the cost of the environmental and other changes such facilities bring about.

I believe that no company, however profitable and however large the contribution it makes to the economy in tax and other ways, should be exempt from using money in the right way. I am not allowed to burn rubber tyres at will in my backyard, because my neighbours are stakeholders in my gardening habits – they want to breathe unhindered. Similar accountability should apply to businesses of all sizes.

That is the Socially Responsible, Triple-Bottom-Line argument, and the machinery to implement it is already in place. For example, the 2000 Race Relations (Amendment) Act requires all public sector organisations to promote equality. Financial organisations might consider making investment funding conditional upon adopting socially responsible practice towards stakeholders. Again, the business case for ethical business is well proven. Here the right use of money is also the 'best' use of money, by a number of practical definitions.

Public money

Public money is sometimes used to promote a community image in ways that do not contribute to the prosperity and well-being of local residents. I know of one Jubilee project in the North that created a highly publicised amenity for a brief time in a location that was then handed over to commercial developers. Local people got no long-term benefits and only incidental short-term benefits. Few local jobs were created, few tourists and local investors were attracted, and it disappeared without trace when the developers moved in. Its chief purpose seemed to be to promote some sort of glamorous urban image. It would have taken only a small shift of planning to turn it into a community project with many community benefits.

Such decisions have repercussions on the business community and also on the social community. Seen from the perspective of the right and wrong use of money, they are hard to justify.

On the other hand, public money is being used in a wide range of ways today that promote communal benefits and local business in ways that benefit everybody. One example is Local Business Partnerships such as that in Rotherham, for example, which has attracted large inward investment, and the environmental regeneration charity, Groundworks. Such schemes are beneficial because they improve the natural and social environment and invite business to be part of a systemic whole: they address questions of quality of life, job satisfaction and environmental protection as well as achieving commercial and financial success for the business members of the partnership.

Some wider issues

If a multicultural society is to be achieved, in which everybody is empowered to realise their potential and contribute their skills, one of the major factors in achieving it will be the right use of money. But ultimately, social change comes from changed people, not from government directives.

The evidence that the gulf between rich and poor is widening, especially in the US, suggests that the capitalist model is fundamentally flawed: capitalism is not working. How can a better way of using money be found?

In 1997, *The Times* featured Chris Webber, UK Chief Executive Officer of SkyNet World-Wide Express, who brought from America an innovative motivating scheme for his sales force (Gray, 1997). He encouraged them to aspire to an expensive lifestyle, personally taking them shopping for expensive clothes and suggesting holiday destinations far more expensive than the ones they would normally choose. Soon they were hooked. Being paid by commission, they had to work harder and harder and become increasingly ruthless in their efforts to close deals, to pay for the new extravagances. Sales rocketed and the company flourished. 'Greed works – it's wonderful!', reported Mr Webber.

I prefer Gandhi:

> The earth provides enough to satisfy every man's needs,
> but not every man's greed!

Greed has been responsible for a large part of the world's problems; but nobody ever caused a problem by sharing their own goods, identifying other people's needs and helping to meet them. It might seem idealistic to propose that Gandhi's creed should be a syllabus topic in business degree courses – but something of the kind is happening, as the business case for ethical practice is increasingly recognised. It is a trend that could become a major influence in business thinking.

The future

Changing embedded attitudes requires determined social reform. We can see it in the huge increase in relational, people-focused, voluntary compassion. Comic Relief and similar projects are one visible symbol of an emerging social trend.

But I want to conclude with another way forward: investment in the next generation. I am constantly astonished and encouraged by young people's capacity for generosity and desire for social justice. I saw it first-hand in Christmas Cracker, a social entrepreneurship project that I co-founded. It ran from 1989 to 1995 and aimed to produce aware and active young global citizens by means of a range of unusual charity projects applying franchising principles to the voluntary sector. The projects were unusual because they applied the resources of established business funding to the innovative and sometimes anarchic ideas of young people (one project devised by the young people, to build the biggest Christmas cracker in the world, attracted £5,000 in sponsorship from companies who saw the media potential of having their logo on the cracker). It was one of the first *virtual* charities, in that it had no physical assets or employees; all operations were outsourced to existing charities, with service-level agreements ensuring delivery and cost effectiveness. Fifty thousand young people took part, 70% of them aged under 25. Its diverse range of programmes generated considerable social capital, both in the £5+ million that it raised from a seed capital of £10,000, and in training young people.

I learned a huge amount from those young people, who themselves provided some of the most creative and innovative ideas. It was a symbiosis that generated massive profits, far beyond the financial.

I began this essay by talking about investment. Projects like Christmas Cracker are extremely good investments. Young people can only grow, and there are many years available for deploying the results.

What is the right use of money? Perhaps the consensus of the faith communities has got it right. Burying it means losing it. Investing it need not mean only a financial return. If money is used rightly, it will grow. But growth might not translate to bigger bank balances. The returns might, in the widest terms, be far more valuable than that.

References

GLA (Greater London Authority) (2003) *Play it right: Asian creative industries in London*, February, London: GLA.

Gray, S. (1997) 'When money is not enough', *The Times*, Travel Section, Premier Appointments, 13 March.

Keynes, J.M. (1932) 'Economic possibilities for our grandchildren', *Essays in persuasion*.

15

Conquering helplessness: ones and zeros

Matthew Pike

Matthew Pike is Director of the Scarman Trust, a national charity
committed to helping citizens bring about change in their community,
in the way that they want.

We have been asked to give our views on how money, private
money in particular, could make people's lives better. An
important and intriguing project!

Immediately, I imagine the various contributors to this book as a
jostling throng of thinkers, writers and doers (in my case all three)
thrown together in Club Class on a jet travelling at 35,000 feet,
tasked with covering whole continents of social, economic and
political considerations; with one eye on the clock.

Meanwhile, far below us, almost invisible under a canopy of clouds,
are the people and communities that are the implicit subject of the
various views and pronouncements here. These people are not
going anywhere. Their perspective is utterly different from ours,
trapped within a syndrome of poverty and powerlessness.

It is for this reason that I prefer to walk. Here, on the ground, the
richness and the poverty of real people's lives shines in starker relief.
Standing here, among the wreckage, it is obvious that while human
lives elude simple nostrums, they can nevertheless elicit powerful
truths that can arm us in figuring out how private money can help
to make a difference.

Living in the wreckage

You could choose any one of millions of lives to reinforce this point. Over here is Shirley, who conducts her profession in the red light districts of South Birmingham:

> "There have been times when I've had my little one in the front seat of my car when I go with a punter ... it's those times I hate who I am and what I do.... But then I go home and open the kitchen cupboard, and all there is is a bottle of tomato ketchup.... I look at my little girl ... and I just sob my heart out...."

Place any two lives like these together at random and you will find all kinds of echoes between them: poverty creates these quirks of solidarity. Here is June, who like Shirley, comes home to a sense of emptiness:

> "Our cooker went and then a few days later, like an answer to our prayers this man comes round with a catalogue and says that I can have anything in it and that I didn't need to put anything down then as a 'gesture of good faith'.... Well I got the cooker, new blinds, and a new confirmation dress for Lisa, and then the bills started coming and getting higher and higher ... they (the loan sharks) have re-possessed pretty much everything now.... I just feel that everything's falling apart and I'll never be able to put the pieces together again as long as I live."

These two stories communicate the most basic human commonplace, that lack of money ruins people's lives. Shirley and June are trapped. Every time they make a step forward, they push up against an invisible wall that squeezes them back again. Faced with this kind of unending resistance, they come to believe (and who can blame them?) that there is nothing they can do to live their lives differently.

You or I, safely installed in Club Class, could easily conceive what might be done. We can imagine giving words of advice. We can see all too clearly the consequences of Shirley's or June's poverty – the impact on mental and physical health, on the chances of a good education or a decent job. But it is one thing to seek to understand 'the issues' from a safe distance, and quite another being down here, doing something, when the whole world is pressing, pressing down.

Lack of money makes tragedies of people's lives, and there are enough Russian novels or Shakespeare plays to remind us that tragedies are never simple. As we think about 'the role of money and markets in promoting social transformation', we forget this at our peril. Easy to pontificate: a hundred times harder to do.

Wrong turnings

So here we are with millions of people whose opportunities to do something or be someone have been gradually withered away. How can we respond? In the past we might have turned ourselves into the cavalry (or indeed into missionaries – like the cavalry but without guns). We might have said, "What a tragedy!" and rushed in to save people in the name of charity.

What we now understand with hindsight, is how this impulse to rescue has so often demeaned and disempowered the very people it sought to serve. We have seen this in the actions of individual voluntary organisations, but the approach and mindset involved has truly been tested to destruction in the actions of post-Second World War welfare states.

Since 1945, governments everywhere have created an increasingly elaborate system of social security for those who had least, based on the simple diagnosis that lack of money was the root problem. At the same time, government developed programmes for whole communities, founded on similar good intentions. Communities were prioritised on the basis of those who 'had least', and the money was found to 'put things right'. The great lesson for us here is how the central role of money was badly misinterpreted in two key ways.

The first fundamental error was the assumption that the beneficiaries of programmes were zeroes to be filled up; 'nothings' to be made into 'ones' through access to more money. There was no acknowledgement of people's intrinsic strengths or qualities. Indeed, the social security system found it immensely hard to show any respect for the human beings that it served. A similar story can be seen in the procession of different area-based community programmes. With each new initiative came a new beauty contest of the marginalised and powerless, each fighting with others to say, "Look over here, look over here, we're worse off than them!".

This presumption that people or communities are zeroes waiting to be turned into ones is a deeply corrosive one. Some years ago it became fashionable to talk about benefit claimants as showing a 'culture of dependency', but the truth, both more disturbing and depressing, is that they suffer from something that can more accurately be called a culture of helplessness. This is what plagues the heads of people like June or Shirley. The more they are castigated or coerced, the greater their sense of despair and desolation.

The first wrong turning to avoid then, is one that imagines that money is the root solution. It isn't. The first stage of the root solution is about people beginning to see those ways in which they are already wealthy, and this takes respect and recognition, trust and love: qualities in which government is not well versed.

But lest this all sounds just too woolly and emotive, we now come to the second key error which is concerned with issues as hard-edged as the first was soft; that is, the preoccupation of business people everywhere: assets, capital, wealth. In other words, ones and zeroes of a different kind.

In the past, government focused upon money in its narrowest form as income and missed the real story, which is that it is assets that really matter in propelling people out of poverty. A large amount of recent evidence confirms that narrow, income-based policies on their own are doomed to failure: incomes are never high enough, and any level once set will always be under political pressure to get it down and keep it down. Furthermore, as the structure of wealth ownership in society as a whole has been transformed through the growth in the property market, the inheritance of property by successive generations and the boom in investment products, the divisions between rich and poor have widened further at ever-increasing rates. It has taken a whole range of guerrilla fiscal measures by the current Chancellor of the Exchequer Gordon Brown just to keep this yawning divide in check.

When we talk about 'assets', 'wealth' or 'capital', people immediately think of financial assets: savings, investments, pensions and so forth, and these forms of wealth are indeed what matter most; but this is not the whole story. It is now widely accepted – from the World Bank to leading UK politicians – that we need to achieve the development of assets in the round, in both their tangible and more intangible forms: physical, human, social, cultural, natural, communications, organisational and knowledge capital, as well as the classic financial products and ownership of land and buildings, and so on.

Ownership of or access to these assets, especially financial assets, conveys a number of key benefits: an ability to cope with setbacks, to look more to the future; a sense of a stake in society; feelings of self-worth and status; an ability to seize opportunities as they present themselves. It has been shown that assets provide a powerful catalyst for civic involvement and entrepreneurial activity of all kinds. Forty per cent of British citizens have expressed interest in running their own business – ownership of key assets make them far more likely to do so.

The central importance of assets is incontestable: the welfare state in practice has often been busy striving to achieve the precise opposite: lack of wealth. All kinds of disincentives have been put in place, for example in respect of permitted levels of savings, which have meant that people had to demonstrate their complete penury, before they could be helped. Similarly, any activity by the unemployed to build income and savings, which might in fact help fund their path out of poverty, is severely penalised. If they do so and ignore the rules, they are transformed into criminals. Turning the most entrepreneurial people into black market criminals is, to put it kindly, a less-than-intelligent public policy.

The role for private money: investing in 'can do' assets

Seen in the light of the range of assets outlined earlier in this essay, communities and people everywhere are already wealthy; they are merely disempowered. Organisations such as my own, the Scarman Trust, exist to reach out to them and promote a 'can do' vision of the resources and therefore the opportunities for action that they already hold in their hands.

Of course, not everyone will move at the same speed. We at the Trust seek out those especially committed, entrepreneurial people, the 'can doers' who can move first and fastest, and who can then bring others along with them, when the moment is right.

At a very simple and basic level, these 'can doers' are talking the same language as the private sector; seeing opportunities, mobilising resources, developing new markets, building a balance sheet – at an individual, organisational and community level. One key opportunity for private money is to invest in these people, with grants, loans, expertise and support, and the unlocking of other forms of in-kind assistance.

As these 'can doers' work and build activities of greater scale, the opportunities for private investment and involvement grows to a larger scale, and becomes gradually more commercial. In the space I have left, I can indicate some brief examples from among a much wider set of possibilities.

Community banks

The poorest in society are often un-banked and crippled by debt. Of clients receiving debt counselling by Citizens' Advice Bureaux in the past year, the average debt burden was £10,700 – against average monthly incomes of just £800. Even those who have escaped such massive levels of debt still find it almost impossible to build any savings. The story of June, above, is a classic example of the despair that this financial exclusion results in.

The financial services industry has withdrawn from many of these communities and, until they re-engage, the problems of poverty will always be with us. It is for this reason that Britain is learning from the evolution of community development credit unions in the US and elsewhere and working to pioneer new community banks, with the potential in Birmingham for example, for 100,000 savers from predominantly low-income groups to be signed up over the next seven to ten years.

Private-sector finance can help bootstrap these new financial mutuals. Ethical investors can make long-term equity and pseudo equity investments that can build capacity and market share among lower-income groups. With growth in participation by a range of more affluent savers and investors (up to a ceiling of 49%), still higher dividends can in time be offered that offer a return on investment that is competitive with many other for-profit investment opportunities. In addition, private-sector financial service providers can offer a whole range of products on a mass basis. By reaching into poorer communities in partnership with a community bank, the costs of acquisition and so on can be reduced, allowing companies to turn an increasing profit from a growing market.

A stake in housing

In 1999, net wealth was £2,752, of which 23% was owned by 1%. The bottom 12 million households have wealth totalling £150. Property ownership has played a key role in this asset inequality. We therefore need new models of housing ownership that are neither pure rental 'social' housing nor pure private. People need ways of acquiring some simple equity stake in the value of their house that can set them on a road to being a property owner in a nation of property owners – nothing else will bridge the gap between the haves and the have-nots in the longer term. It is for this reason that many are now calling for a new style of mutual ownership of housing.

As with community banks, private long-term investment can greatly increase the value of local physical assets and public investment here so as to expand the opportunity for those on low incomes to gain a foothold on the property ladder. As property markets in run-down areas begin to take off, so a larger quasi mortgage industry could take off, supporting the acquisition of housing equity stakes.

Social investment

The examples of both community banks and approaches to housing equity show the role that private-sector finance can play in making existing public and community resources go further and be much more productive – from both a social and an economic perspective. Both are exemplars of the way in which a fundamentally investment-led approach can be extended into every corner of social and economic policy, offering both financial and social returns.

The challenge is as formidable as the opportunities are huge. Every possible chance must be seized to direct money as investment to build assets and secure financial and social returns of all kinds, from individuals, organisations and whole communities.

In part this will take some product innovation. We need micro loans of varying rates, from 3% APR to 18% for a host of purposes. As sketched out earlier, we need long-term, 'patient' investment. Tools such as pound-for-pound incentives for saving among low-income groups need to be universalised. We need money that is paid in relation to clearly measured social outcomes. But the product innovation will have greatest impact as it transforms the way that government itself operates.

One example of wholesale change that is possible is the social security system, which as I have said, undermines wealth accumulation and creates a culture of helplessness. The benefits system should therefore be turned into a social investment service. Actuarial analysis of a type that insurance companies practice on a daily basis could tell the government what an individual is likely to cost them on 'the dole' over future years. They could therefore calculate quite easily the value for money of a more generous investment in skills or enterprise development, and so on.

However, cultural change is not just a one-way street. Government can also act to shape the ways that markets operate in profound ways so as to ratchet up the value for everyone engaged. A classic opportunity lies with the pensions industry: there it is in the doldrums, a victim of its own speculative bubble. At the same time, we have public infrastructure starved of investment – with the Private Finance Investment ill-suited to address more than a small proportion of the overall finance required.

What the government could do is establish a Social Finance Investment programme. It could establish a not-for-profit company tasked with sourcing pension fund investments from individuals and ethical fund managers. The programme would offer a guaranteed long-term return of say 9% to pension holders and direct finance to programmes of public works. This could save the government the equivalent of 5p on basic rate income tax, allowing taxes to be cut or public services to be improved, according to the priorities of the day.

An invisible handshake

Adam Smith, the classical economist, talked of an invisible hand guiding the efficient operation of markets. Too often in practice, markets act as an all-too-visible fist, exacerbating the effects of structural inequalities and the failures of past government policies.

The future, in contrast, is all about an invisible handshake between private investment and the forces of social progress. The latent wealth and entrepreneurialism within communities must be unleashed. Private investment can fuel this activity, achieving still greater multiplier effects by transforming the way that government operates through a true investment culture.

In this way we can build a market place that delivers on Adam Smith's original vision: one that combines greater equity with increased efficiency, and one that builds the wealth of all individuals, organisations, communities and society as a whole.

16

The myth of easy money: developing financial services that would really help

Niall Cooper

Niall Cooper has been National Coordinator of Church Action on Poverty since 1997. He is also co-founder and chair of the Debt on our Doorstep campaign, a network of local and national organisations committed to securing 'fair finance' for those currently experiencing financial exclusion in the UK.

We live in an era of fantastically cheap money and easy credit. Unless that is, you are poor. One of the cruellest paradoxes about the use of money within the modern market economy is that those who have least pay most. That is nowhere more true than in relationship to money itself.

As we are all too painfully aware at times, the UK economy is awash with cheap money. Interest rates remain virtually the lowest they have been for decades. Even unsecured loans are available for less than 10% APR (annual percentage rate). Household borrowing now amounts to over £150 billion – greater than the total debts of the 49 'least developed' countries, which inspired thousands to join the Jubilee 2000 campaign in the late 1990s. Is this a sensible way of sustaining demand within an otherwise sluggish economy, or a foolish credit bubble? Clearly, for the majority of UK citizens, credit is now a way of life, and a convenient means of enabling 'us' to buy anything from foreign holidays to this week's supermarket shop.

However, my main concern is not the implications of the scale of borrowing on the wider economy, or on the whys and wherefores of over-inflated levels of consumerism, although both are cause for concern. No, my question in relation to the right use of money is quite simple: why should those who have least pay the most?

> Ironically, concern about financial exclusion has arisen not because more people cannot gain access to financial services but because use has increased, leaving a minority of people on low incomes behind.
> (Kempson, 2002, p 9)

There are 13 million people in Britain struggling to exist on low incomes. By that we mean as little as £107 a week for a single person and £188 a week for a lone parent with two children.

> The National Consumer Council and others have shown people on low incomes frequently pay more than the rest of us for the 'privilege' of access to many of the essentials of life: gas, electricity, water, phone bills, and even food. They do so because they prefer, or are stuck with payment methods and supplies that are more expensive. (Klein, 2003, p 3)

One of the main underlying problems is that companies seek to 'cherry pick' the most profitable consumers, who in many cases are also the more affluent, with regular monthly salaries, high credit ratings, and the ability to pay by direct debit (thereby reducing the companies' collection costs). The flipside is that disadvantaged consumers are frequently offered less attractive deals, required to pay up front, or premium prices for their preferred (or required) payment methods. In many cases they are also prevented from switching to a better deal because of debts incurred. More vulnerable consumers are not protected from being targeted by unfair marketing practices which can result in them switching to a worse deal.

However, nowhere is the 'excess cost' of being poor greater than in relation to money itself.

Whereas I, a salaried professional, am able to borrow money at less than 10% APR (and if I manage my credit card well, at 0% APR), my neighbour who may be living on a fraction of my income, may well be paying anything up to 800% APR for 'short-term' credit.

Over one and a half million households lack even the most basic of financial products. Over three million are unbanked. Almost eight million people are judged by the institutions that make these decisions to be un-credit worthy and would be refused access to mainstream credit (Datamonitor figures reported in New Economics Foundation, 2002).

This is not to say that such people do not need credit. Quite the opposite. If you are living on a 'tight' budget, your need for credit is all the greater. How else can you cope with the 'uneven' nature of household expenditure (birthdays, school uniforms, Christmas) let alone the 'unforeseen' events (a broken cooker, a funeral to attend at the other end of the country)?

In the words of one woman who attended one of Church Action on Poverty's Policy Forums on debt:

"I have a fifteen-year-old daughter and she needs clothes so I have to get a 'Provi' loan or vouchers. It's hard. At the end of my benefit I've nothing left to pay back the loan and vouchers. I can't spend money on shopping and bills." (Participant at Church Action on Poverty National Policy Forum, 9 July 2001)

Since the deregulation of the consumer credit sector in 1974, and the abolition of the ceiling on interest rates, there has been a mushrooming in the 'alternative' credit market, to fill the gap left by the mainstream banks, building societies and other myriad purveyors of cheap credit. (There are now upwards of 1,500 different credit cards available within the UK market.)

Chief among these is home credit. Home credit involves lending relatively small amounts of money (although £500 is not such a small amount, if your weekly disposable income is less than £100), and collecting repayments on a weekly basis. It is a perfectly 'tailored' product, designed to cater for people living on a tight weekly budget, managed in cash and accounted for down to the last penny. The only problem is the cost: anything from 170% to 800% APR (and in a few cases even more).

If this were a small, unlicensed back-street business affecting a few dozen people here and there it would be one thing. But it is not. Home credit is big business: the sector as a whole is valued at over £3 billion, and serves more than three million customers each year. The market leader, and by no means the worst of the bunch, is Provident Financial plc, one of the UK's top 100 companies, with profits of over £160 million last year.

Now, of course, Provident Financial will tell you that when borrowing small amounts of money over short periods of time, the APR is 'meaningless'; that the cost of credit has to reflect the high costs of weekly collections; that they are lending at the most 'risky' end of the market; and that other forms of credit available to low-income households are equally expensive. (Provident Financial have produced figures to show that their costs are comparable with those of unauthorised overdrafts and home catalogue companies.) All of these things may contain more than a grain of truth, although the evidence of an independent chartered accountant does not appear to support their case (Murphy, 2003, p 3).

The plain fact of the matter is that, if you are poor in the UK today, you will pay way over the odds for access to money. And that cannot be right.

The effect of borrowing money at 170% APR is to reduce the purchasing power of every £1 borrowed to just 70 pence. Not only do people on low incomes have less to start with, but the pound in their pocket is worth less as well. The impact of all of this on individuals, families and whole communities is incalculable.

"I don't think anyone can understand properly just how it feels, to dread letters coming through the letterbox. When they did come you'd feel so ill you'd put the letters behind the mantelpiece – never even open them sometimes."

"At the moment I'm on income support and child benefit. I've used the 'Provi' and Shopacheck and I've been unable to keep paying them so I don't do that no more. Now I have to buy from shoplifters so I have money to look after myself." (Participants at Church Action on Poverty National Policy Forum, 9 July 2001)

Such personal testimonies are corroborated by evidence compiled nationally from Citizens' Advice Bureaux (CAB) across the country.

> CAB debt clients often reported that the impact of debt on their lives
> had been devastating. A quarter of CAB debt clients were already
> seeking treatment for stress, depression and anxiety from their GP.
> Clients reported that relationship breakdown, feelings of isolation and
> the stress of living on a tight budget had affected them deeply.
> (Citizens' Advice Bureau, 2003, p 3)

The shadow of debt falls not just on individuals and families, but also on whole communities. A community survey carried out on just two streets in Meadow Well, North Shields, found that 87% of all households had loans with doorstep lenders. On average, households were paying out a third of their weekly incomes (which only amounted to around £200 per family in the first place) in debt repayments. When these figures are multiplied up for the whole of the Meadow Well estate, it was estimated that around £5 million a year is being paid out in debt servicing and repayments, and that interest payments alone amounted to over £1.6 million (Cedarwood Project Community Debt Survey, 2002). Communities such as Meadow Well can ill afford to shell out such enormous sums of money, in what amounts to a huge drain on the local economy. And it hardly makes sense of neighbourhood renewal policies for government to be pouring millions of pounds into communities, when significant sums are then siphoned off in debt repayments and extortionate charges. Not, in my view, a right use of money.

In previous generations, the language of debt was very different to today. Usury and debt slavery may seem old-fashioned terms, but they represent strong moral and social tradition of antipathy to debt and those who would entrap others in it. In the *Divine Comedy*, Dante portrays the usurers as anti-social and puts them down in the seventh circle of the Inferno, sitting on burning sands with cashboxes around their necks, condemned for being violent towards others. More profoundly, the Judeo-Christian tradition equates debt with slavery. (For more on traditional attitudes to debt, see Swinson, 2003.) In the Book of Genesis, the Israelites' exile and enslavement in Egypt was a direct consequence of debt and economic misfortune

> Our money is all spent.... There is nothing left.... Buy us and our
> land in exchange for food. We with our land will become slaves to
> Pharaoh.... (Genesis 47.18-19)

So what can be done? Would it not be a right use of money to
make cheap credit available to those who need it most?

There is a clear case for tightening regulation of extortionate
lending, and for some form of legal ceiling on the levels of interest
and other charges that can be charged. Interest rate ceilings apply
in various forms in Germany, France, many US states, Canada,
Australia, and indeed, most developed Western economies. But
greater regulation alone will not achieve the desired outcome.

> Without action across government, tighter regulation alone could
> make matters worse. To be effective, tougher legislation needs to be
> combined with support for initiatives that widen access to affordable
> credit and money advice. (New Economics Foundation, 2002, p 24)

There is plenty of evidence that, much like the rest of the population,
people on low incomes need access to a range of financial services,
many of which they are currently excluded from entirely, or have
only limited access to – and at a price.

A survey of residents in a poor neighbourhood of Bristol in 2001
found that people aspired to save but frequently needed to borrow.
They were attracted to schemes that link saving and borrowing,
giving them access to low-cost loans. However, they often needed
to break the cycle of borrowing from high-cost lenders to be able
to start saving. There was a widespread mistrust of banks, insurance
and credit companies and a high level of disengagement from
financial services. Asian residents faced problems, as most financial
services do not comply with the teaching of Islam (Whyley et al,
2001).

The researchers concluded that needs for financial products and
services in deprived communities are best met by a combination of
national provision with a local presence and city-wide 'one-stop
shop' services run in partnership between national providers and
local organisations.

Why does it prove so difficult to provide financial services to meet these needs? Is there some iron law of nature that says that making affordable credit, money advice and budgeting services available to those who need them most is the wrong use of money?

Credit unions, as mutual savings and loan cooperatives, provide a fantastic vehicle for mobilising the savings and assets of the whole community in an equitable and inclusive way. Surely a right use of money? Yet less than 1% of the UK population are currently members of credit unions.

Our near neighbours in the Irish Republic manage things differently. Walk up virtually any high street, from the largest town to the smallest village, and you are likely to see the offices of the local credit union. Indeed, almost half of the Irish adult population are members of credit unions.

Clonmel Credit Union, serving a small town in South West Ireland, has over 16,000 members; provides loans at 0.875% per month (around 10% APR); and also offers a wide range of financial services to its members including savings protection and an annual dividend on savings; life savings, loan protection, death benefit insurance; house, contents and car insurance; and mortgages. Should you wish to make a visit, they also offer bureau de change facilities, rail tickets and hotel discounts.

Not satisfied with this, the Irish government also funds a national Money Advice and Budgeting Service, with over 60 centres across the Republic, providing access to high-quality money advice, financial literacy training, a special budgeting account (set up via the local credit union) to enable weekly payments into an account, from which outstanding debts and regular bills can be paid by direct debit and standing order.

In contrast, efforts to apply notions of the 'right use of money' to tackle financial exclusion on this side of the Irish Sea are currently decidedly half-hearted.

While there are a number of government and other initiatives in this area, they are currently piecemeal and uncoordinated: the 'Savings Gateway' to promote savings by low-income households, which is currently being piloted by the Treasury, actually excludes the involvement of credit unions. Money advice services are offered only on a patchy basis, and frequently in isolation from any other services (in contrast to the Irish money advice and budgeting service);

a number of national 'financial literacy' schemes have been established, which may promote increased 'literacy' but do not address the lack of choices available to people on low incomes (especially in relation to sources of credit). And crucially, no government department or statutory agency has any direct responsibility for promoting access to affordable credit, in spite of this being a central element of financial exclusion. (For a more detailed critique of government policies on debt and financial exclusion see Church Action on Poverty, 2002.)

At the local level, a significant number of schemes to promote access to savings and credit have emerged in recent years: credit unions, though tiny in comparison with Ireland, do provide over 300,000 members with access to affordable savings and credit. While some credit unions are struggling with the new regulatory regime introduced by the Financial Services Authority in 2002, others are now growing rapidly and developing as robust social businesses. Over 70 housing associations are involved in promoting financial inclusion in some form or another, and some have established specific (mostly arm's length) savings and loan initiatives. A number of Community Development Finance Institutions, most notably in Portsmouth and Salford, have established schemes to provide access to affordable credit to those on low incomes.

However, to date, most of these schemes are relatively small scale and have been developed by local social entrepreneurs, with only mixed levels of support from the statutory sector. Only a handful offers services to more than 1,000 individuals.

The situation is crying out for some 'joined-up' thinking, a bold strategy to mobilise the strengths and assets of the public, private and community sector, and indeed people in poverty themselves, to end poor people's reliance on extortionate lending, and to put easy and affordable credit within the reach of those who need it most.

"People are still trapped in debt and poverty. When will change come?" (Participant at Church Action on Poverty National Policy Forum, 9 July 2001)

References

Cedarwood Project Community Debt Survey (2002), unpublished.

Church Action on Poverty (2002) *Forgive us our debts*, December, Manchester.

Edwards, S. (2003) *In too deep: CAB clients' experience of debt*, London: Citizens' Advice Bureau, May.

Collard, S., Kempson, E. and Whyley, C. (2001) *Tackling financial exclusion: An area-based approach*, Joseph Rowntree Foundation.

Kempson, K. (2002) 'Life on a low income', *How people on low incomes manage their finances*, London: ESRC.

Klein, G. (2003) *Life lines: The NCC's agenda for affordable energy, water and telephone services*, National Consumer Council, September.

Murphy, R. (2003) *The case for an interest rate cap in the UK*, London: New Economics Foundation/Child Action on Poverty, June.

New Economics Foundation (2002) *Profiting from poverty*, December, London.

Swinson, A. (2003) *Root of all evil? How to make spiritual values count*, Edinburgh: St Andrew's Press.

Part Five: Conclusions

17

Promising approaches and mechanisms

David Darton

From all sorts of perspectives, the short chapters in this book suggest approaches that governments, organisations, both private and voluntary, and individuals might take to ensure that money is used as effectively as possible to achieve social objectives. There are also suggestions for how our monetary and economic systems might be developed to facilitate this. Here I summarise some of the approaches suggested.

Changes to our financial and economic systems

- A more transparent system would allow buying and selling to be acts of social responsibility rather than acts of self-interest. This could include making social and environmental costs explicit in pricing through introducing appropriate taxes (Jonathan Dale), or creating a price system that makes the use of natural resources explicit (Pierre Calame).
- At the whole economy level, replace gross national product (GNP) with an index of economic welfare to make social and environmental gain as important as financial gain (Jonathan Dale).
- By providing the information and motivation that allow 'full-value' investment decisions to be made, the total blended value of economic gain, social gain and environmental gain would be maximised (Jed Emerson).
- Assemble better information to back up corporate social responsibility claims so that consumers know where to invest (Tony Stoller).

- The law should be changed to create stakeholder companies rather than shareholder companies (Jonathan Dale). Firms should return value to all stakeholders, not just shareholders (Jed Emerson).
- Expand the concept of fair trade to include not only benefit to the consumer and producer, but also take account of costs to society and the environment. At a more macro level, make trade relations fairer in this sense by ending agricultural subsidies in developed countries (Jonathan Dale).
- Begin a national debate on relative pay and rewards in order to provide the climate for slowing the relative income growth of the rich and increasing the relative growth of the poor (Polly Toynbee, Moraene Roberts). Introduce sectoral wage councils to set sectoral minimum wages above the national minimum wage that are as high as possible (Polly Toynbee).

Government action

- Create a giving culture by going beyond current attempts to make charitable giving more attractive in tax terms. Some mechanisms to achieve this could include earmarking some income tax for charitable giving, introducing public service for the young (possibly rewarded with a small pot of cash for them to give to charity), and 'incentivising' all employers and educational institutions to ensure that a certain proportion of money and employees' time is given to good causes (Julia Neuberger).
- Mend mistrust in government so that people feel that higher taxes and more collective spending will effectively deliver those collectively provided things that are so critical to our quality of life (Polly Toynbee).
- Remove disincentives to save from the welfare state and disincentives for the unemployed to undertake activity: failure to do so turns the most entrepreneurial into criminals (Matthew Pike). Ensure that policies are made from a premise that values contributions other than employment (Moraene Roberts).
- Raise public sector pay (including contracted out) for those at the lower end. First, persuade the public that rising public sector pay is actually a good thing. It would encourage low pay in other sectors to increase. Reducing wage inequality is the only

sustainable way of significantly reducing the low incomes of the poorest (Polly Toynbee).
- Encourage trade and enterprise when giving aid; it should not be just a hand out (Stephen O'Brien).
- Improve service delivery in areas such as the support that social services give to keep families together by ensuring that sufficient resources are put into developing real knowledge of the struggles of disadvantaged people and that decisions are based on respect for the human rights of all people (Moraene Roberts).

Business and other organisations

- Accept a moral – as well as profit – basis for business decisions. Avoid the search for short-term advantage by ensuring the ethical or religious grounding of organisations (Tony Stoller). For there is not always a business case for corporate social responsibility and philanthropic motivations are often in the long-term interests of business stakeholders (Philip Collins).
- The best mechanism for companies to express philanthropy might be to give to charities rather than try and manage their own, often-confused, 'social responsibility' activities that try to relate to a business case (Philip Collins).
- Take a long-term view in investment decisions rather than a short-term financial market view. Firms and voluntary organisations should employ pension fund and investment managers who are able to take this long-term view (Pierre Calame).
- Have workers on boards to help reduce current norms in the differential between the highest and lowest pay in an organisation (Jonathan Dale).
- Invest in 'can do' people. Ensure that profit opportunities are exploited in poor communities (Matthew Pike). Invest in social entrepreneurship (Ram Gidoomal).
- When thinking about how to help disadvantaged communities, ensure that you are aware of their full range of assets – physical, human, social, cultural, natural, communications and so on, as well as standard financial ones (Matthew Pike).
- Spend what is necessary in time and money really to understand the perspective of those living in disadvantaged areas (Matthew

Pike). Listen to and understand the worldviews of those you are trying to help (Dorothy Rowe).

Financial institutions

- Introduce and expand a range of financial services that can help disadvantaged communities: for example, community banks; bootstrap new financial mutuals. Ensure that micro loans are available, covering the full range from, say, 3% to 18% (Matthew Pike). Products should relate to poor people's needs, such as ones that link savings and borrowings. There should be tighter regulation to prevent excessive interest rates and widen access to affordable credit and advice (Niall Cooper).
- Encourage further development of credit unions and better access to money advice and budgeting services (follow the case of Ireland) (Niall Cooper).
- Ensure that financial institutions have ethnic sensitivity, with minority language services and products that relate to cultural requirements for savings and investment, such as need to create dowries (Ram Gidoomal).
- Introduce financial services that empower borrowers. Rely more on trust and honour. For example, support zero-interest bonds and see if the *hoondee* system – that is, community lending under-written by trust and guaranteed by *izzat* (community honour) – can be extended, for example, through group syndicate borrowing (Ray Gidoomal).
- Take investment decisions on the basis of what can make resources go furthest – that is, investment that increases a community's assets in ways that levers in more. Establish a social finance investment programme with guaranteed long-term return to encourage pension and other fund investment in poor communities (Matthew Pike).

Voluntary organisations

- Facilitate new forms of housing ownership. In particular, voluntary organisations should explore mutual ownership of housing (Matthew Pike).

- Foundations should tackle governance issues rather than adopt a 'doing-good' project approach – that is, what sorts of systems should be developed to allocate goods and services not appropriate to market allocation (Pierre Calame).
- By using all their instruments, foundations should demand social as well economic gain from recipients, grants, and the provision of venture capital funds. Charities could manage their accounts through community investment banks rather than mainstream accounts that take no account of social value (Jed Emerson).
- Take the time to develop knowledge of a person's struggles and efforts and the problems that bring them into the scope of a voluntary body's activities (Moraene Roberts).

Individuals

- Determine what is 'enough' in terms of money in order to free each one of us from being a volunteer slave to employer or profession. This can help stop money being the symbol of success and allows other things that relate to a broader definition of quality of life to become more important (Charles Handy).
- Recognise that money is not a neutral force. Our decisions relating to money need to take serious account of the needs, wants, desires and expectations which have already shaped the assumptions of our cultural context (Church of England's Doctrine Commission).

Money and the financial institutions and markets that underpin its exchange are, of course, not intrinsically evil, in need of automatic constraint; but nor are they an unambiguous good.

Hopefully, the ideas that have been explored here will contribute to a debate about the approaches that will ensure that money contributes to *positive* social change. Firm conclusions may then emerge about the practical policies and actions that can be taken as modern British society continues to change in the coming decades.

Index

NOTE: Page numbers in bold indicate a chapter by that author.

Y

young people
  charity work 111–12
  easy life 56
  public service 58
Yunus, Mohammed 107

Z

zero–interest bonds 106–7, 138

To order further copies of this publication or any
other Policy Press titles please contact:

In the UK and Europe:
Marston Book Services, PO Box 269
Abingdon, Oxon, OX14 4YN, UK
Tel: +44 (0)1235 465500
Fax: +44 (0)1235 465556,
Email: direct.orders@marston.co.uk

In the USA and Canada:
ISBS, 920 NE 58th Avenue, Suite 300,
Portland, OR 97213-3786, USA
Tel: +1 800 944 6190 (toll free)
Fax: +1 503 280 8832,
Email: info@isbs.com

In Australia and New Zealand:
DA Information Services, 648 Whitehorse Road
Mitcham, Victoria 3132, Australia
Tel: +61 (3) 9210 7777
Fax: +61 (3) 9210 7788,
E-mail: service@dadirect.com.au

Further information about all of our titles can be
found on our website

www.policypress.org.uk